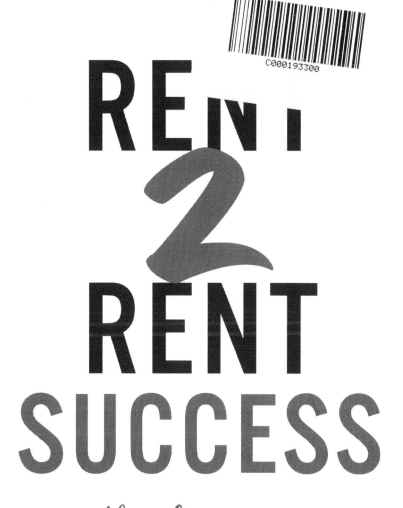

RENT 2 RENT SUCCESS

Our *ethical* 6-step system
to get you started in
property without buying it

STEPHANIE TAYLOR
& NICKY TAYLOR

DOUBLE DASH PRESS

Published by Double Dash Press, 2021
www.doubledashpress.co.uk

Produced, designed and edited by Known Publishing Ltd

ISBN 978-1-8383532-0-9

CONTENTS

PART 1

RENT TO RENT REVEALED:
A PEEK BEHIND THE CURTAIN
17

PART 2

HOW TO BECOME A RENT TO RENT ROCKSTAR:
DISCOVER THE RENT 2 RENT SUCCESS SYSTEM
87

PART 3

BEYOND WORDS:
TURN YOUR COMMITMENTS INTO ACTIONS
263

"

You are a star.

It's your time to shine.

It's time to stop
waiting.

You're ready now to

Believe Bigger,

Be Bolder, and

Be a Gamechanger.

THIS BOOK IS FOR...

... you, if you have the spark for more than the nine to five. If you'd like more freedom in your life. If you'd love to get started in property but feel you don't have enough time, money or knowledge to get started. This book will show you how.

RIGHT NOW YOU ARE:

, Feeling fed up having to spend so much time working
, More focused on what's really important to you and the importance of quality time with family and friends you love
, Aware of the fragility of relying on a job.

YOU WANT TO:

, Feel less worried and more confident about your financial future
, Spend fewer hours working so you can spend more time with your family and people who matter to you
, Maximise the money you do have in a low-risk way and make it work harder for you
, Have the freedom to indulge the passions you don't have time to enjoy now.

You're looking for something sustainable which lasts. You're not looking for a get rich quick scheme. It's important to you to contribute, to deliver value, and you definitely:

-   Don't want to be involved in anything sleazy or unethical
-   Don't want to take big financial risks
-   Don't want to move forward without a proven plan.

Ultimately, you would love to be free to work less; to choose what you do, where you go and when you take your holidays; to take an unexpected afternoon off when your children need you, or to spontaneously add an extra day onto a long weekend trip; to be free to begin building up to funding a fun retirement, making a difference and leaving a legacy.

You are a Star.

You're reading this book because you know that it's your time to shine. It's time to take the success you've already achieved and spread it to property and wealth creation. It's time to stop playing small, stop hiding and stop waiting.

If you're ready to Believe Bigger, Be Bolder and Be a Gamechanger, this book can change your mindset and, when you take action, it can change your life.

THIS BOOK WILL...

... show you the laser-focused proven strategies that we use with our students to get moving in property fast. It will show you how to get your first rent to rent property up and running. It will show you how to increase your belief and give you the tools to start taking action.

We have distilled the key principles we teach students in our Rent 2 Rent Kickstarter Programme into this book. You may be surprised by what is possible for you right now with the resources you already have. And we'll show you how you can work less, have more and be more financially confident about your future.

It's not just about getting your first property. It's about taking that big step forward towards financial freedom – whatever that means for you. Whether it's the freedom to spend more time with your family, the freedom to give up a job you'd rather not spend 40+ hours each week doing, the freedom to travel, or the freedom to be a gamechanger, to make an impact, to leave a legacy. Whatever it is for you, getting started in property is going to help take you there.

ROCKSTAR ESSENTIALS!

To help you get even more out of this book, we've added essential resources such as checklists and templates you can print out and exercises you can do. These will help you get better results from the book. You can access them at **rent-2rentsuccess.com/essentials**.

Our passion is to help you realise that Yes You Can! Most people don't know how to get started in property without a lot of money or time or experience. Most people struggle through life working in jobs that don't fulfil them, investing their precious time fulfilling other people's dreams.

That was us, too, and we simply wouldn't have believed that there was an ethical way to make money from properties we didn't own. And that is why we wrote this book. There is a simple way to make a good living that doesn't take 40+ hours of every week and 40+ weeks of every year.

We're excited to show you how to get started building a consistent cashflow without buying a single property. We're going to guide you through the exact same six-step Rent 2 Rent Success System that we use.

Welcome to Rent 2 Rent Success. Your journey to living life your way begins today. And you don't need huge amounts of money to get started.

Everything you need for success is already within you.

The first step is simply to learn the system for success, and believe it is possible for you. Our wish for you is that you realise it before we did!

The second step is to read and take action on everything we are laying out for you in this book.

The third step, if you are really serious about making a change, is to download the **Rockstar Essentials** we've put together that complement this book.

We would have loved to put everything you need in here, but some things don't lend themselves too well to book format; they are much more useful in the way we've produced them in **Rockstar Essentials**, such as worksheets, checklists and templates you can print out and exercises you can do. These will help you get better results from the book. You can access them all for free at: **rent2rentsuccess.com/essentials**.

PREFACE

'I had to make my own living and my
own opportunity. But I made it! Don't sit down
and wait for the opportunities to come.
Get up and make them.'

Madam C J Walker

As I looked around the room, I was shocked. Our interior designer, Rohanna, looked at me expectantly. I could hardly take it in. What a transformation. Where once you could hardly see through the grimy and rotten sash bay windows, which had been painted permanently closed, now I stood looking at them, beautifully restored, bathed in light and overlooking the cathedral. Where once the spindly, mismatched and downright ugly kitchen units had stood with doors missing and hanging off, a beautiful new kitchen gleamed in the light. Where once the dark, rubbish-strewn room with stained carpet told a story of sadness in this place, here I stood in a gorgeous room I'd be proud to call home.

I felt as though I couldn't catch my breath or speak. This is a position I never thought I'd be in. This studio is one of 12 units in the property. Ten studios like this one, plus a two-bed flat and a shop, in a beautiful four-storey listed building opposite a cathedral.

Photo: After Refurbishment

See more photos on the website: rent2rentsuccess.com

As I stood there that day with Rohanna, taking in how beautiful the rooms were, I started welling up. I was reminded of how far I'd come. The way things started for me, I just never thought I'd end up here.

The journey from teenage mum on benefits to business owner, property investor, published author, podcast host, speaker and coach has been a long and winding road. Back in those days, I wouldn't have imagined I'd have been in *Entrepreneur* magazine or have articles in *The Telegraph* newspaper.

Things have changed dramatically for my sister Nicky and me since we got started in property full-time in 2016. We learned the little-known strategy of rent to rent and it's changed our lives beyond all recognition. In the last few years, we've had business and financial success which has far exceeded what we thought was possible when we started.

We:

- Built a thriving rent to rent HMO (houses in multiple occupation) management business with contracts worth over £2m
- Systemised our business and employed staff
- Started Rent 2 Rent Success to help others achieve success
- Bought property worth over £1m.

And here I am standing in one of our properties with Ro, with tears in my eyes because I didn't know this was possible. I didn't start until I was 45 and I am amazed by what has happened in a few short years – but what if we'd started 10 years ago or 20 years ago? All those years I struggled financially as a single parent. If only I'd known.

I knew I had to write this book so that more people *do* know. So that *you* know.

'When you've worked hard, and done well, and walked through that doorway of opportunity, you do not slam it shut behind you. You reach back, you give other folks the same chances that helped you succeed.'

Michelle Obama

PART 1

RENT 2 RENT

A PEEK BEHIND THE CURTAIN

Discover the ethical way to get started
in property without buying it.

"IF ANYONE EVER GETS
IN YOUR WAY AND TELLS
YOU NOT TO FOLLOW YOUR
DREAMS... DO NOT BE
BURDENED BY WHAT HAS
BEEN WHEN YOU CAN
CREATE WHAT SHOULD BE."

Kamala Harris

'I WAS LIVING TO WORK, NOT WORKING TO LIVE'

'The biggest adventure you can take is to live the life of your dreams.'

Oprah Winfrey

So many of us strive for career success and find that it's not what we expected. On one level, 'success' is great with a well-paid role, status at work and in your family and community. Often the problem is that you're earning money you don't have time to enjoy. And the other things that are important to you become relegated to a 'someday' that never happens. Worse still, the people most important to you – your partner, your children, your wider family and your friends – only get what's left of you after work has taken its more-than-full-time bite.

It's 'normal' to rely entirely on one source of income. It's what most people do. It's seen as 'safe'. When you get a new job, your friends and family will celebrate with you. When you start a new business, many of your friends and family will warn you about the risks you are taking.

In many of us, the need to maintain the status quo of a nine to five job is blended with a potent mix of fear, hesitation and imposter syndrome, stopping us from getting started and keeping us 'stuck'. Even though you are very talented, you too might not be able to see the potential within you. And that is certainly true of Nicky, my talented sister. I'm so proud of her and what she's achieved in her career. We both started from the same humble beginnings and Nicky really took off – yet, as you'll learn, she was still hampered by imposter syndrome.

Nicky and I created this book together. You'll see as you learn more about us and read our Success System that it's a blend of our talents. I'm Stephanie and I'm usually in front of the camera while Nicky is behind the scenes making sure everything happens as it should. I am the one writing the words on these pages, so I'm the *I* in this narrative. But this book is a gift from both of us. The words are mine, but Nicky's love and caring is here on these pages too.

Nicky hasn't often told her story publicly, and I feel proud to be able to share it with you here. It's one you may be able to relate to: the experience of giving your all to your career and leaving the field of play feeling bruised, battered, exhausted and underappreciated. Nicky will tell her story in her own words.

NICKY'S STORY

'I left school at 16 to study chemistry and accountancy at college. All my friends had plans, careers that they had dreamt about for as long as they could remember, and I had... well... nothing. I didn't know what I wanted to do. So, my hastily made plan was to go to college, then uni, then become an officer in the British Army. Why an officer in the army? Because Dad had been a Staff Sergeant in the Royal Corps of Signals. Indeed, I was born at RAF Wegberg Hospital in Germany. And why accountancy? Because that's what Dad did after leaving the army.

But within three months, I'd dropped out of college. I really didn't enjoy my time there; because I was at college in the absence of a plan that inspired me, there wasn't enough incentive to keep going.

It was 1989, and soon after I dropped out of college, I started a government Youth Training Scheme as an administrator. I was earning £30 per week, which wasn't very much, even back then. Once the scheme ended, I quickly found a role at a local bakery as an accounts assistant. Bright-eyed and bushy-tailed, I set to work in the only way I've ever known how to do: very hard. Very diligently.

When I was taken on, the Managing Director promised me a bonus if I met all my targets. I exceeded them. Blew them out of the water. I took great pride in being the best that I could be at work, learning and delivering far beyond what would have been expected from someone in my very junior role. Somehow, I found the courage to ask for the promised bonus, but it was clear from the reply that my boss had never intended to make good on his promise. That was a painful realisation for me: no matter how hard I worked, there was no guarantee I would be fairly rewarded. What hurt more was being let down by people I admired and trusted.

Eventually, I left the bakery and went on to work for other companies. As I looked around me at work, I became scared. What I noticed was that people were unhappy in their roles. Yet they stayed in them forever, sticking with their routines, and that was their existence forever and ever, Amen. Being in that environment drains you. It takes your energy. It takes your skills away. With that new realisation, I also became aware that, if I wasn't careful, my whole life would just be as it was in that moment. And that's when I decided I needed to move on.

I pondered what I could do. I decided to leave Birmingham and move to London, where one of our aunts lived, and that's when my career began to fly, going from the backwaters of Birmingham to the cut and thrust of banking administration in London between 1998 and 2014. My 16 years in banking were both incredibly rewarding and soul-destroying.

Here I can just touch on the surface of these experiences and share a few of the lessons and learnings that eventually brought me to property.

My diligence, commitment and willingness to put in 15-hour days as the norm, even when no one was watching, meant that in every contract role I took, I was offered a permanent position or the contract was extended and extended. I rose quickly through the ranks, from Assistant Payroll Co-ordinator to Assistant Manager of Payroll, to Assistant Vice President – Payroll Manager, to Vice President – HR Administration Manager, to Head of HR, to HR Operations and Recruitment Manager, to Global HR Business Manager – HR Director.

Throughout my early career, I often felt I might have been viewed as 'less than' because I didn't choose to do a degree. So, if you also feel you're not good enough because you don't have a degree, I hope this will encourage you. After coaching hundreds of people, I have yet to meet someone who doesn't have self-doubt, no matter their educational status or achievements. It's made me realise that if I didn't have a lack of a degree to worry about, I'm sure I'd have found something else.

Working for the Big Four investment banks, I was recognised as a rising star many times. My life outside of work, though, mainly involved sleeping and recovering from work. I led large teams; in fact, I had been responsible for all HR administration for over 11,000 employees. As you can imagine, this was stressful. It was life-limiting. But the most painful part was going from being on Top Talent and Rising Star programmes to being made redundant, which happened three times over a 16-year period.

Typically, I would overdeliver beyond all targets set for me, have an incredible relationship with my team and management. Then a new manager would come in, perhaps wanting to bring their own teams in, 'restructure' the department, and make my role redundant. Even though it is the role that is made redundant rather than the person, it feels intensely personal, especially when you're putting your heart and soul into your work. Perhaps you can relate to this. Feeling you're contributing something important to the company. Feeling you're supporting a team that also supports you. Helping your company, which reciprocates in salary and in support to you. Only to find that the rug can be pulled out from under you at any moment and your loyalty was misplaced.

The first time I was made redundant, it absolutely devastated me. It knocked me for six. Afterwards, I had a career break because I just couldn't function – I was in shock. I'd given everything. I'd achieved exceptional results in the role, generated multi-million pound savings for the bank. I'd been highlighted by managers as a top performer, was part of the talent programme, was achieving beyond my targets in every review. But they could just kick me to the kerb whenever they wanted to, whenever my face didn't suit, or I didn't fit the new structure.

It was the third of these instances that made me take stock of my life. Even when life was good at the bank, it was bad.

I'd leave home at 8am to catch the train and tube to Canary Wharf, and take the last train home after midnight. And this was my daily routine, rather than the exception to the rule.

I was working hard, but I was sacrificing life for work, putting in very long days for a fancy title: Director, Vice President, Global Head of this or that. Earning a good salary but feeling frustrated and uninspired, realising I was living to work and not working to live. That's fine when you're passionate about your role, and I could see I was delivering tremendous value for my bosses and my employer, but it became extremely unsatisfying and frustrating for me. I felt tied to it. I felt like it wasn't a choice. It had just become my normal.

And being made redundant was a huge blow. Again.

I knew it was time for more life in my life. After 16 years in these highly stressful large financial services firms, I'd had enough and decided to take a very different path.

The role I secured was Director of Business and Operations at a new school. I thought a role in education would be perfect, although it would mean a drop of over 60% in my salary. I thought it would be a good fit for me for three reasons:

I had so many transferrable skills.

It would allow me to give back to my community, which was a huge driver at that point. I'd be moving away from shuffling numbers and reports and going to meetings to make the bank richer, and into a role that would really make a dif-

ference: I would be part of an ethical organisation and help invest in our children, in our community, in our future.

Very importantly, it would give me a better life. After all, schools aren't open 15+ hours per day. They close at 3.30pm. And, as if life couldn't possibly get any better, they close for six weeks in the summer!

Later, when I talked to some of my new friends in the Education sector, they hooted with laughter when I explained how I thought education equalled work-life balance and six weeks' holiday.

My transition from Banking to Education can be characterised by three words. Frying. Pan. Fire!

Just as 2020 brought for many a new-found or deepened respect and appreciation for our NHS, 2014–2016 opened my eyes to our amazing Education sector. Schools are political pawns, always having to jump to the latest ill-conceived idea thrust upon them by the government with no extra money and diminishing year-on-year budgets. And schools are expected to be so much more than just providers of education. They have to wear so many hats – parents, police, social workers, doctors – and they have to do it all in the public eye whilst taking care of their own mental health and well-being for comparably very low salaries.

As Director of Business and Operations in the school, I was responsible for everything that was not teaching related, so that would be all the financials, HR and payroll, fundrais-

ing, procurement, facilities management, cleaning, catering, safety and security. You get the picture. I was even required to be a cleaner when there were any... er... mishaps in school, as our cleaners didn't arrive until the end of the school day. Let's just say that those cleaning jobs were often unpleasant!

My days grew longer as the school's senior leadership team took it in turns to arrive in time to open the school at 7:30am to welcome the children. (It is a progressive school with longer opening hours to help working parents.) After two years during which my working days crept up to 17 hours, including most weekends and working through school holidays, I was exhausted. But the school was in a fantastic position, with new policies and procedures and fully trained staff, so it was ready to go. I knew for my well-being and sanity I needed to move on.

This period is summed up by the fact that, after a year of being repeatedly told there were no funds for additional staff to support me, when I left my role I was replaced by THREE members of staff!

I decided to take time for myself, go on holiday, take stock and think about what I wanted for my next chapter, so I flew to Jamaica for three months on my own. I realised that, although I'd done well in my career, it had happened to me. I hadn't chosen what I'd wanted for my life. In many ways, it felt as though I'd given so much of my life away. I pondered which direction to go in next. I thought it might involve property as my own home had gone up so much in value after refurbishment.

Whilst I was away, Stephanie encouraged me to read the famous book Rich Dad Poor Dad *by Robert Kiyosaki. Not being an avid reader, or frankly a reader at all, this was bottom of my list of things to do in Jamaica. But one day, in the absence of a better plan, I reluctantly decided to purchase the audio version of the book and press play as I relaxed on the beach. Six hours later, I had a new clarity, a new focus and a new vision. I felt excited by the possibilities and the opportunities that now started to sharpen and come into focus. I definitely wanted to do something in property and definitely wanted to be my own boss. It was time for my work ethic to drive and realise my own dreams rather than my employer's.*

Photo: Nicky enjoying Hellshire Beach, Portmore Jamaica

When I returned from Jamaica to the not-so-sunny Becken-ham, Kent, I was still excited. But by then the reality of not

having a job or a regular income was also starting to hit home. My toddler brain went into overdrive and started screaming:

What are you doing?

Get a (bleep bleep) job!

How are you going to pay your mortgage?

You're not good enough to run your own business.

You can't make enough money to cover all your bills and out-goings and mortgage.

What are you thinking?!

I started to do what I've done so many times before with so many other ideas; slowly but surely, I realised I was scared. Scared of not showing up for myself. Scared of not being good enough. Scared I wouldn't be able to do what would be required.

When I was in Jamaica, listening to a book on the beach in the sun, it was easy, and so clear; I thought, 'yes, I can do this'. Back on my own at home in grey Beckenham, with bills on the table, I found it harder to work out the 'how'. Even something as simple as having a lodger and turning my own home into an asset, I resisted for a long time. My mind and my thinking just weren't in the right place.

But it was as though the stars had aligned, because it was when I'd just arrived back from Jamaica that Stephanie and I chatted in my kitchen – and what we discussed has made the last few years so different from the previous decades.

Looking back, what shocks me is that, in spite of managing multi-million pound budgets and overseeing operations for thousands of employees, I wouldn't have had the confidence to start in business on my own. There I was, competent and hard-working, delivering first-class results for every company I worked for, saving them millions, yet still, I was questioning my abilities.

I had the spark of an idea that I wanted more. And, like so many of us, I massively underestimated my ability to do it.

––––––––––––––––––

Nicky had the spark. You're reading this book because you have the spark too. You're part of the 5%. You want more for your life. You want to live life on your terms. You don't want the sort of 'safety' that sucks the life out of your soul, that drains your health and makes you wonder 'what if?'

What if you had a way out that was tried and tested?

What if you could get started with little money?

What if you could minimise risk by doing it on the side of work to begin with?

That's what this book is about. The ethical system to create a new future for yourself in property.

Working nine to five is not always the safe option, and for many of us it's not the easy option either, with long hours, high stress and negative health consequences, both physically and mentally.

My story is very different from Nicky's, and yours may be too. You may not have had Nicky's level of career success; I didn't. In the next chapter, we discuss how we came together.

'I COULD DO THIS MYSELF. I COULD DO IT MUCH BETTER SIMPLY BY ADDING CARE.'

'No matter where you are from, your dreams are valid.'

Lupita Nyong'o

'It's all right for you, Steph, because... '

, You run successful businesses.
, You have your own multi-million pound portfolio.
, You know the right people.
, You're confident.

This is what people often say to me before explaining why they couldn't possibly get started in property. As humans, we're a strange lot. When we see others achieve success, our first instinct is to look for reasons why we can't do it. Well, it was easier for them because... they're younger, they're older, they have fewer children, don't have an accent, know how to rollerblade, have a dachshund...

The reason we do this is because it seems easier not to try! But is it easier not to try?

For a small percentage of people, there is a simmering frustration in going to the office every day and in doing things that, for the most part, they don't want to do. In asking for holidays, in worrying about office politics, in not having enough time to spend with your family. In knowing another path is possible and wilfully not taking it. And the chances are high that, if you're reading this book, you're ready for a change and you're ready to take action.

You want more than what nine to five life offers. You want to work on your dreams, not your boss's. You want time for your family and the people you love over and above those you spend most of your life with at work.

My own story is one of decades 'wasted'. Years spent living too timidly and aspiring to too little. Years spent wanting to 'blend in' and not put my head above the parapet. It's a story that, to be honest, for many years I did not want to share. I felt that if people knew it, they would look down on me. I was so afraid of what others would think, and I was ashamed. I felt so badly about myself, and was convinced others would too.

Now I've seen the other side and know what it means to have founded businesses that have created homes for hundreds of people, with revenue of over three quarters of a million pounds each year, and that have been featured in the media. I know it's just as doable as working nine to five and feeling unfulfilled. Both have their unique opportunities and challenges, but for me the opportunities in running your own business are so much more exciting and fulfilling than the frustrations of a nine to five. If you feel the same way, it is open to you, too.

I mentioned in the preface that I became a mum as a teenager. I was 18. My son Alex was such a happy baby; he was open and loving and chatty and friendly right from the start, and I wanted to be a good mum and do the best I could for my beautiful, gurgly baby boy. I tried to be the best mum I could.

I was convinced that the best way for me to look after us both was to get a job to support our little family of two by working full time. The trouble was, with no A levels or work experience (I became pregnant at college), and little confidence, the low-paid admin jobs I was doing barely paid for the childcare I needed. I took little baby Alex out into cold dark mornings at 6am, walked to the nursery and then caught the bus to work, before returning on cold dark nights at 6pm. It was soul-destroying.

Bizarrely, I felt I was doing the right thing. After a while, though, I started to feel torn: was this the right thing? What finally made me see the light was that Alex seemed unhappy at nursery. A simple conversation with a member of nursery staff about Alex's baby milk (which I was expressing) drew a look of disgust; it was only on her face for the briefest of moments, but I saw it there and it finally made me realise. The staff didn't care about him as much as I did. It felt in that moment that they didn't care about him at all. It became so obvious. The benefits of working were unclear, and I knew I'd be more valuable to Alex at home.

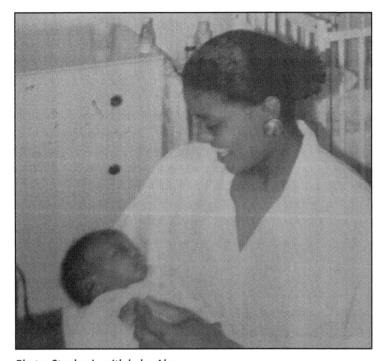

Photo: Stephanie with baby Alex

I decided to stay home and look after Alex myself, and that was a blessing. We are lucky in the UK to have this option. I didn't feel lucky, though; I felt ashamed. Being on benefits brought with it an extra dose of low self-esteem. Standing in a queue at the post office each fortnight to collect government Income Support payments, I'd hand in my book and receive cash payments. It was a world full of small humiliations.

What I used to find particularly stressful was grocery shopping. I received £48.90 per week Income Support and Child Benefit, in cash. I can vividly remember walking around the supermarket, choosing carefully with my calculator (this was well before smartphones!) in order to avoid the indignity of not having enough money at the till. Those times I wanted the ground to open up and swallow me as I decided what to leave behind, seeing the eyes of those behind me offering a mix of impatience and sympathy.

As Alex flourished at home with me, I signed up with the Open University to study for a degree, which gave me an incredible feeling of achievement. I loved learning and waiting for the textbooks to arrive in the post before writing my essays long-hand; that was how most people did things then. Then I'd eagerly await the results dropping through my letterbox with detailed notes from my tutors.

It turned out I was exceptionally good at writing essays and was achieving first-class marks consistently. I was thrilled to focus my mind on learning and analysing and debating, and I was surprised to find that other respected people thought I was good at it. Alex's zest for life and loving ways, aided by the intellectual outlet of learning and the help and support of my family, helped me through this time.

When Alex was older and went to school, I went to university full time and ended up getting three degrees in all! I loved learning, and it gave me the flexibility I needed for family life. We had some wonderful experiences together in those years of tight budgets and hand-to-mouth living, like our very first holiday abroad together to the island of Zakynthos.

I was excited to eventually move into full-time graduate roles and surprised to find that the 'prize' wasn't the life I'd dreamed of. The roles weren't as well paid as I thought they might be, and the lifestyle was not great, either. The school holidays were a challenge. Life still felt like a struggle.

This book is not all about me, though – it's about you. And my story, like yours, has many twists and turns. These include starting up my own 'business'. The Sunday Brunch Club was a social network where people paid to be members and I organised holidays, events and everything from book clubs to art clubs. It was fabulous. I built a great network of people, many of whom became good friends, but I didn't understand processes, outsourcing, or how to grow the business beyond me. Eventually, after seven years, I'd burnt myself out. A particularly stressful Hogmanay Ball was the final straw. And in January 2013, I sold the business on to another member of the Club. Lessons from this experience helped us systemise HMO Heaven from the start, and now we want to share that with you so you can have a high-cashflow business that doesn't become a full-time job or leave you on the brink of burnout.

After recovering a bit, I started to do temporary minimum-wage jobs. This was a strange choice; I had three degrees, I'd run my own business, so why did I feel I had nothing more to offer?! Looking back now, I can see that I felt like a failure and that I wasn't worthy or capable of a 'professional' role, so I sought out vastly underpaid temporary administrative roles instead. It seems ridiculous now, but I see so many others undervalue what they can offer too.

Eventually, I had the opportunity to interview for two positions at an engineering firm. One was an office manager role, and the other was as an admin assistant. Even though I'd previously run my own business, I was unsure whether I'd be able to do the office manager job. I remember being hugely excited by the opportunity for a more demanding role than the reception roles I'd been doing, but also very anxious that I simply wouldn't be able to do the office manager role, although I wanted it so much. I'd already had some crushing disappointments where I'd been unsuccessful in securing very low-paid receptionist positions, which had further dented my spirit. I felt useless and of little value.

After my interview, I was like a cat on hot bricks, pacing back and forth in my mind. On one hand, trying to find reassurance that I hadn't made a fool out of myself by aiming so 'high' and, on the other, trying to convince myself I was more than capable of being an office manager.

When I heard from the agent about the role, it felt like a knot in the pit of my belly. It was as though time stood still. If I got neither role, I'd know I was worthless; if I got the admin role, I'd know I wasn't good enough yet, and if I got the office manager role, I'd know I'd 'arrived'... I got the office manager role! And things started to change for me.

As a side note, it's so easy to see, looking from this distance, that I was easily capable of the role. What if my self-worth wasn't tied to a role and what others thought me capable of? What if I could become unshakeable in the face of any disappointment? That is something all successful people need to have: the ability to move on past disappointment to success. I'll talk about this shift more in Mindset Mastery, where I discuss how I went from this very fragile state to the way I feel now. I am now able to deal with any disappointment or unexpected challenge because I know I will support myself, I will be resourceful and I will keep going.

After the call, I was ecstatic, but this quite quickly gave way to anxiety. I didn't know what to do. What if I couldn't do it? I tortured myself for hours... then I eventually decided, right then and there, to work it out. It wasn't brain surgery or rocket science. I could learn it. I'd take my notebook with me, find out what they needed to happen, and then do it. Or find out how to do it. I didn't have to know everything on Day Zero; I could be resourceful. That simple thought gave me the courage to go through with it rather than call the agent back to explain I was a fraud who had no place becoming an office manager!

I got my mojo back. I enjoyed the office manager role, setting up a brand-new office and creating a hub for field engineers. Eventually, I began to find the role too small and too repetitive; I felt I could tackle something more demanding and, let's be honest, better paid. That's when I found contracting in the financial services, where the day rate was the same as the weekly pay in my low-paid temping roles. It was mind-blowing to me that, for very similar work, the pay was so much higher. And the contracting bank roles were actually less demanding in many ways, as the focus of responsibility was much narrower. I received the clear message that higher income didn't necessarily require harder work. Doing specific things increases your income more quickly.

I was content with life, although I admit I found the world of banking stuffy and suffocating. I found the office politics impossible to navigate. I disliked the high-pressure environment and the way the most unimportant things were turned into life-or-death situations. The long hours. The ridiculous number of unnecessary emails. In fact, after a while, the whole thing felt unnecessary. What was I actually doing at the bank? It wasn't fulfilling for me. And, more fundamentally, the role I was in didn't make use of my talents.

Most likely, though, I would have stayed in financial services contracting until retirement had it not been for one phone call. Because, with so many failures to look back on, I know I wouldn't have had the courage to try property if it hadn't been for the call that changed everything; the everyday happening that changed my world.

My mum telephoned me one sunny morning while I was getting ready for work in my beautiful Harbourside flat in Bristol. Getting ready for the onslaught that was life at the bank. Mum didn't call me in the mornings. Mum rarely asks for anything, and that's why I should have taken it more seriously.

Mum was ill. She tried to sound upbeat, but I could hear that she was scared. She called because she needed the reassurance we all need when we feel sick and anxious and afraid. I feel so ashamed because I was worried while we were on the phone. Yes, I was worried about Mum, but I was also worried about work. I was worried about being on time, and the project meeting, and the presentation, and and and… and so many other things that seemed so important at the time.

That was the day something changed for me. As I sat at my desk that afternoon, it hit me like a punch in the belly. It was the moment that I let myself see what my heart already knew. My mum was scared and alone in Birmingham and I still went to work in Bristol. I should have been with my mum – nothing was more important than that. Not the projects or the project meetings or the deadlines or the presentations.

It came to me with clarity that day that the bank would be absolutely fine without me, but my mum wouldn't be. Do the things we insist are so important actually mean anything to us and our lives? I'll bet there are very few people who, on their death beds, wish they'd spent more time working at a bank. And there are countless millions of people all over the world who wish they'd realised sooner how to create the freedom to live a life they really want, with more time for their loved ones.

For me, that well-paid contracting job at the bank was like a prison. I needed the work to fund a lifestyle I didn't have time to enjoy. What if Mum was really ill and I wanted to go to Birmingham for months at a time? What if Mum was well and I wanted to enjoy more time with her?

What hit me that day was that I wanted to be able to choose to prioritise my life and focus on the people and things that mattered to me the most. That's when I knew that I had to make flexibility my reality. I needed more freedom. I wanted a passion and a vision and a proper life, not just a job. That day, I made making the leap a must, and I finally committed to feeling the fear and doing it anyway.

I was still tentative, though; it's one thing to commit to oneself, but it's another to put that commitment into practice. What exactly would I do? With so many failures to look back on, would a business really work for me? I didn't think I had the right skills to be successful. However, fuelled by a fire in my belly, telling me that I must make a change, I knew that the time was now. I was 45, and time wasn't standing still!

I pondered on it, wondering which way to turn or how I could make anything work, and it came to me: property! It seemed an easier type of business to understand. I didn't feel I needed to be Lord Sugar or Sir Richard Branson to do it. After all, I knew of 'ordinary people' who were full-time property investors and no longer worked nine to five. This gave me a little spark of an idea to find out more, even though it seemed like a mysterious world, and not one for people like me who didn't have £50k in the bank, or the right contacts or the right knowledge.

I started attending property events to find out more, and I was utterly amazed by what I saw. People who had left their jobs and found success in property – massive success, way beyond what they could have achieved in their jobs. And as I expected, there were strategies requiring what seemed like massive amounts of money, hundreds of thousands of pounds, to get started: things like development projects and new builds.

What shocked me, though, was how many 'ordinary people' stood up to tell us about their journeys from the nine to five to financial freedom. And I learned that there are ways to get started in property with little money. You don't need tens of thousands of pounds in the bank.

I remember the moment when the penny dropped for me. I was sitting listening to the speakers at a property networking event in Bristol. I was in the front row. My jaw was on the floor. I was amazed by what the speakers were saying. They were impressive, yet also so real. So ordinary, and yet so extraordinary.

As each of a series of properties came across the huge screen, the speakers explained how many thousands of pounds their company had made over the contract after all the costs

"

I knew I could do

it better simply by

adding care.

had been taken out. £30k; £50k; £75k. The list of properties seemed to go on and on. So many stories. So much money.

They called it rent to rent; they were explaining how to make money from properties you don't own. Normally, I would not have listened. I would have thought it a scam, or told myself it was for people with lots of money. That's for property people. That's for business people. I might have said, 'Well, it's OK for them, but not for people like me.'

But things were not normal for me any more.

I had so many reasons not to act. I was confused and afraid of failure. I just didn't believe in myself enough. As I sat there on 21 March 2016, after the gut-wrenching realisation that I needed to change, I decided right then and there that I could, and I would, and I must. I had failed at so many things in the past. It was only thinking about Mum's call, and how I'd been living my life all wrong, that gave me the strength to try.

Rent to rent was the perfect model for me because I felt certain I could do it. After all, it's managing a property. As a mum, I knew how to manage a household, and I'd started a business before and managed demanding professional roles. I saw people managing house shares very badly and not caring. I knew I could do it better simply by adding care. I was inspired to do it in a way that would be a win-win-win for our landlords, for our housemates and for us. That's where the name HMO Heaven comes from; I wanted to transform HMOs from hellish to heavenly.

It was at this point that my sister, Nicky, returned from her holiday in the Caribbean (and mercifully stopped sending me photos of herself relaxing on beaches all over Jamaica while I was stuck at my desk in Bristol!). We stood in her kitchen in Beckenham with a cup of tea.

I gushed about rent to rent and explained that I'd set up a limited company the month before and was already starting to look for properties. Because Nicky is very cautious, it hadn't crossed my mind that she would want to jump straight in; I thought perhaps she might get involved in one property deal and then maybe, over time, become more involved. But she surprised me by saying she wanted to jump in 50-50 right from the start, so we decided to join forces – and HMO Heaven, our rent to rent business, truly started.

Mum is fine now. In fact, she's better than fine. She's in her seventies and has a new zest for life. A few years ago, she was having problems with her knee and I thought walking might help her. I bought us all a Fitbit (a fitness tracker watch that counts your steps and lots more), and we had a family leaderboard. Nicky and I faded away after a year or so, but Mum is still going strong, walking over 20,000 steps every single day. I'm so proud of her dedication. She feels younger and healthier than she has in years. We spend more time together, too. Mum is looking after our gran, who is in her nineties; at the moment, she wants to stay in Birmingham, but our business means we know that, when Mum is ready, we can buy her a house here. In fact, we're already on the lookout for one.

My son, Alex, is now in his thirties! I'm so proud of him. It's been so thrilling to be able to share with him our knowledge of property over the last few years. He conscientiously saved for some years and has bought his first home, turning down our frequent offers of financial help. It needed a back-to-brick renovation, so it was a baptism of fire for him! With his own property in the bag, we're excited about what the future holds for him in terms of building on his assets and growing what he has and what he can contribute. It makes my heart sing to know that I can help guide Alex to achieve financial independence whilst also being able to support his family (if he chooses to have children) and leave a legacy. It's a gift most people won't ever achieve.

Photo: Stephanie, Mum, and Nicky

We show our children through our own example. I could not show what I did not know, and Alex grew up in a home of love but also of scarcity. I'm so glad I know now. I'm grateful to be able to live this life of abundance now and to share that with him. And with you. It's a joy to feel each day that I'm doing what I'm meant to be doing.

Nicky and I have achieved business and financial success that I would have found hard to imagine beforehand. But we know this is just the start. I waited until I was 45 to start HMO Heaven. I want to show that you can start where you are with what you have and achieve incredible things. To show that Yes You Can get started in property with little money, little time, and little experience.

Now, let's move on and talk about what rent to rent actually is.

WHAT IS RENT TO RENT?

'It's not knowing what to do. It's doing what you know.'

Tony Robbins

I n this chapter, you'll learn the real magic in the rent to rent model for residential property and how it can work for you. You'll discover:

1. **What rent to rent is**
2. **The three ways to do rent to rent**
3. **A real life example of how it works in practice.**

Most of us can see that property is a route, but feel we don't have enough time, money or knowledge to start. And if you're reading this book, I know that working ethically is important to you. This is why we started teaching what we know, because so many property 'trainers' have a sleazy approach; we wanted to show that there is an ethical way to make money out of properties you don't own, whilst providing value for landlords, for housemates and for you and your business.

If you feel sceptical, that's natural – I did, too. You were interested enough to read this book, so I invite you to open your mind to the possibility that rent to rent success is achievable for you too.

WHAT IS RENT TO RENT?

We truly love the elegant simplicity of this business model.

The heart of it is this:

- You rent a property, usually for three to five years.
- You pay the owner or letting agent a guaranteed rent, and usually you take on paying the bills.
- You rent the property out to tenants for a higher rent than you're paying the owner.
- The difference between the rent you receive from tenants and the rent you pay the owner or letting agent, after the property running costs, is the profit that you make for your business.

It's an incredibly efficient business model, as it:

- Requires little money to start up
- Means you can be profitable within a few months (most businesses are not profitable in the first year)

"

There is an ethical
way to make
money out of
properties you
don't own.

- Gives you consistent recurring cashflow (most startups do not have recurring revenue)
- Gives you the names and addresses of your perfect customers (most businesses have to find their customers).

 And I love the fact that, at its very simplest, it is just renting a property – something thousands of people do every day.

We focus on HMOs (houses in multiple occupancy, or house shares) and I know there is confusion about what HMOs are. Before we move on to the three ways to do rent to rent, let's look at what HMOs are in more detail.

What is an HMO?

A property is a house in multiple occupancy (HMO) if both of the following apply:

- At least three tenants live there, forming more than one household.
- A toilet, bathroom or kitchen facilities are shared between housemates.

A property is a large HMO if both of the following apply:

- At least seven tenants live there, forming more than one household.

, A toilet, bathroom or kitchen facilities are shared between housemates.

A household is either a single person or members of the same family who live together. A family includes people who are:

, Married or living together, including people in same-sex relationships

, Relatives or half-relatives; for example, grandparents, aunts, uncles, siblings, step-parents and step-children.

All HMOs in the UK with five or more people now require a licence. Let's move on now to the different ways you can do rent to rent.

THE THREE WAYS TO DO RENT TO RENT

House shares or HMOs

This is where you rent out a property as a house share, so you rent each bedroom separately. It's what many people know as a student house share, where each person has their own bedroom and then shares a kitchen and bathroom, although HMOs may have en suites or individual kitchenettes.

You could take a property being let out to a single family and rent it out by the room. A two-reception, four-bedroom property, which might rent to a family for £1,000 per month, may be converted into a five-bedroom HMO by using one of the reception rooms as a bedroom, with rent of £600 per month per room – equivalent to £3,000 for the month. Although you would usually be paying the bills in an HMO, the cashflow is significantly higher from an HMO than a single let.

We'll explain more later about how we work almost exclusively with properties that are already HMOs. This way, we don't need to make all the changes required to change a family home into an HMO, which can be both time-consuming and costly.

Our aim in what we do is to provide a great service for house-mates – a beautiful, affordable home they love to live in.

It wouldn't work, though, if it didn't also work from a business perspective. The great thing about HMOs is that when you match the right 'product' to the right customers, there is always demand. Even in a market downturn, people need somewhere to live. And especially in a market downturn, people love that house shares provide an easy 'all bills included' option. Even in our post-coronavirus world, the desire to house share has actually increased. We're experiencing higher demand than before the coronavirus pandemic.

HMOs produce consistent recurring revenue. Each housemate commits to staying with you for at least six months, and many stay for much longer. The cashflow is much higher than from a single family let, too – so you need fewer properties, as we will discuss in Model Magic.

With this much higher cashflow, HMOs are hugely attractive from a business perspective, but what puts people off is that they're more time-consuming to run than a single family let. And that is true. What's also true, though, is that with a few simple systems in place, you can run an HMO business in a few hours a month. As you'll see later, as few as three to five HMOs can easily produce enough profit to replace an average UK salary.

Serviced accommodation

Here, you'd take a property and typically rent it out by the night as a whole unit rather than by the room. For example, a two-bedroom flat, which might rent for £800 per month, would rent for £50 per night. This is equivalent to £1,520 for the month, if the property is rented every night.

People get very excited about serviced accommodation when they see the potential income. However, the costs are also high; they include the same bills you'd have running an HMO (gas, electricity and water), plus other costs like laundry and cleaning, and fees for online booking portals, which are around 15%. Then there's the VAT of 20%, which decreases profit (there is no VAT on rent, so rent to rent HMO and single lets are not affected by VAT).

At first glance, serviced accommodation looks hugely attractive with its higher revenue but, as I mentioned above, the costs are much higher too. Serviced accommodation is a hospitality business with guests. It's more time-intensive, more costly to run, and has more marketing requirements, as you're constantly looking for new guests. And it can be high stress, as having five-star ratings is very important in attracting guests.

Not only that, but occupancy can be unpredictable. To make higher cashflow, you need to have guests for most of the month. This is difficult to forecast with any certainty, especially when you're new to it, and some areas have planning restrictions like the '90 day rule'. For example, since 2015 you are only allowed to provide short-term lets in London for up to 90 days in a calendar year. So, many people find that they actually lose money in the first year, in spite of the fantastic income.

Single let

Mostly you'll be using one of the strategies above – either HMO or serviced accommodation.

Once you get started in rent to rent, though, you may sometimes be asked to manage single let properties. When I say single let, I mean a property rented to a single household, such as a couple or a family. Typically, single lets require less management, although the potential for cashflow will be lower. I've included this so you know it's an option – it's not something we choose to seek out, but it's an extra we can offer to our HMO landlords who have single lets they'd like us to manage.

Single lets are straightforward, but usually, the cashflow is much lower, so it'll take much longer to reach your business goals.

This book focuses on the HMO strategy as it's simpler for beginners than serviced accommodation, takes much less time, and is less risky.

Rent to rent HMO gives the best return on time and money invested.

When I was starting out, I would have read something like this and thought, 'this just doesn't sound possible for me'. I think many of us feel that way in the beginning.

A REAL LIFE EXAMPLE OF HOW IT WORKS IN PRACTICE

LOISE WILSON'S STORY

For over 20 years, I dreamed of getting into the property business. But as a busy working mum with a successful career as a corporate accountant, it was always on the back burner and it didn't ever seem like the right time to start.

Should I risk leaving a successful career to pursue my dream? Where would I begin in the property world? Where would I get the funds to invest in properties? Property just didn't seem accessible to someone like me, and it was very rare to see females in property.

I also think what really gave me the confidence to try property was when I was asked to run a local charity, a food bank, for our church. Even though I did not have any direct experience of running a food bank, I used all of my previous management knowledge and skills to navigate my way through. The food bank became a greater success than I could have imagined, which made me revisit the idea of property once again.

I realised that if I could make a thriving success of the food bank and learn it from scratch, then I could start in property too, even though I knew nothing about it. I had the confidence in other areas of my life and brought that to property. I knew I could learn it.

With this in mind and a new-found confidence, I took the leap and quit my job to pursue my property journey. My Cosy Homes was born, and I am so glad that my dream is now my full-time reality.

Loise found her first two properties in Croydon, London. They were already HMOs, partially tenanted and in good condition, so she only needed to spend money initially on refreshing the two empty rooms and getting the properties ready. Then, over time, she spent a further amount on refreshing some of the communal areas. Now Loise is making over £1,400 per month after all costs on the two properties.

Photo: Nicky as a baby with Stephanie and Mum

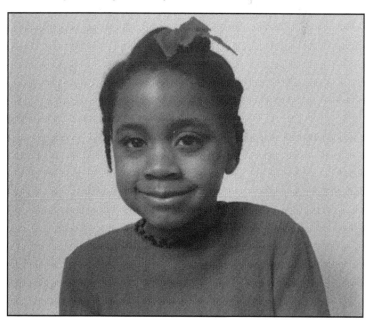

Photo: Nicky within 5 years

WHY FIVE IS THE MAGIC NUMBER

As every parent knows, five years go very quickly and a lot can change in that time. Look at what happens over the first five years. Little Nicky has grown so much compared to little baby Nicky above. She has skills and abilities that just a few years ago didn't exist for her.

It's the same in property. Take the steps and, within a short time, your life will change a bit. Within five years, it will have changed a lot. And that is where the magic happens.

Let me show you.

Let's take Loise's first property as an example.

- Profit after costs:
- Every month £715
- Every year £8,580
- Every five years £42,900

That's amazing, isn't it? For a few hours work each month, Loise earns a significant extra income. This is *after* all the costs have been taken out.

So the question is: can you imagine how amazing it would feel to have your first property? Imagine telling your family, friends, and colleagues, all the doubters, that it really does work. **How would it change your life if you had an extra £42k of income over the next five years?**

So, let's just stop for a moment.

With just three properties, even at an average £500 profit per month. that is £18,000 per year, which for some people is a full-time UK salary, for a part-time business. Yes, you still have to pay tax on the income, just as you do with your salary – but incredibly, the cashflow on three average properties adds up to £90,000 over five years.

How many properties would it take to make you financially free?

 To replace an average UK salary, it's between three and five properties

That's the power of rent to rent.

RENT TO RENT MYTHBUSTERS

'Whatever they say you can't
do, do it twice!'

Angie Le Mar

Most people don't know about rent to rent, and those who do know about it often regard it with suspicion. When I first came across it at the age of 45, I thought: 'this can't be right', 'this sounds like subletting', 'surely it's not legal', and 'why have I never heard of it before?!'

So, I'm excited to get stuck in here now and bust the most common rent to rent myths people ask me about. I have looked through the questions we get asked in our Rent 2 Rent Strategy Sessions,[1] the questions people ask in our Rent 2 Rent Success Secrets Facebook group,[2] our YouTube channel,[3] and the messages I get about *The Rent 2 Rent Success Podcast*.[4] Here, I'm going to bust the most common rent to rent myths I hear.

Isn't it subletting? And isn't subletting illegal?

Most people just can't believe that rent to rent is a legitimate business model. Let's get this one sorted straight away.

Yes, rent to rent is legal.

Perhaps your forehead is still furrowed, so I'm going to explain a little more. Rent to rent has been used in commercial property since the pyramids were built. OK, maybe not that far back, but almost. Commercial leases are long-term leases that give a commercial property tenant (usually a business) the right to sublet a property. Typically, these are 'full repairing and insuring' leases, where the tenant takes on all the costs of repairing and insuring the property. This is what the rent to rent model is based on.

This model came over into residential property and has been adapted to give residential landlords similar guarantees to the ones that commercial landlords enjoy. Northwood is the biggest guaranteed rent letting agent in the UK, with over 85 offices; it started as a single office in 1995.

Subletting simply means 'leasing to a tenant'.

The reason why some people think rent to rent might be illegal is that subletting has a bad name. Subletting usually comes to public attention when it's in the news because someone has done it illegally without the knowledge of the property owner. That is absolutely *not* what we advocate.

Rent to rent *is* legal when it's done with the full knowledge and consent of the owner and when the correct contracts are in place. (We'll come on to contracts in Make the Deals.) If you still have an eyebrow raised and are thinking 'well, she would say that, wouldn't she?' you might be swayed by the fact that rent to rent is recognised by the UK government's Property Ombudsman, the Property Redress Scheme (PRS).

The Property Redress Scheme's definition of rent to rent:

> Rent to rent is where an individual or company, known as the agent, rents a property from a landlord for a specified period of time, during which the landlord receives a fixed guaranteed rent from the agent. This can be attractive to landlords who want a hands-off investment with guaranteed income. The agent then lets the property, generally on a room-by-room basis, and manages the property.[5]

The fact that so many people dismiss this strategy out of hand means there's more opportunity for you. What you know and act upon will change your income and your impact.

Critics may grudgingly admit that it is in fact legal, but still wonder 'why would a landlord give a property to me?'

Why would a landlord give a property to me?

This is the second most popular question I get asked. People are incredulous when they ask, 'Why would a landlord give a property to *me*?!' They add an exclamation mark to the question mark with their tone of voice.

They understand how rent to rent works, they accept that it's legal, but they absolutely draw the line at believing that any landlord or letting agent would give a property to them. If this thought had crossed your mind, you're in good company; it crossed mine. And most people I work with have the same hesitation. It just doesn't seem plausible that a landlord would walk past a traditional high street letting agent and choose you, who likely have little or no property experience.

And yet people are getting their first properties from landlords and letting agents every day. People without prior experience, without property and without huge pots of cash in the bank.

How?

The 'secret' is that HMO landlords and letting agents have problems you can solve. When you learn how to describe your solution effectively, you become an irresistible option to your perfect customers. There are examples of people getting their first deal right throughout this book and in the series of Rent 2 Rent Rockstars interviews[6] on *The Rent 2 Rent Success Podcast* and YouTube channel. In Magnetic Marketing, we'll delve into this and share what to do to attract landlords and letting agents to work with you, even though you're new.

Why would a letting agent want to work with me? Aren't I a competitor?

This one really flummoxes people because, well, 'aren't we competing with letting agents?' But letting agents, like everyone else, will help you get what you want when you help them get what they want. Agents want to have their fees paid, their rent paid and their properties looked after with minimal risk and no hassle. All of which you offer.

The great thing about working with agents is that they have properties coming to them all the time, which means that so can you! Rather than you going out and looking for deals, they'll come to you. In Magnetic Marketing, we go into detail with some case studies to bring this to life for you.

Don't you need lots of money to get started in rent to rent?

Businesses often take tens of thousands of pounds to get started. But as we talked about earlier, rent to rent is an efficient business model which allows you to get started for less than you might think – and become profitable before you might think, too.

In Mind Your Business, I walk you step by step through everything you need to set up your rent to rent business legally, ethically, inexpensively and quickly. And on our **Rockstar Essentials website** I've indicated the current price of each item; it actually costs under £600 to get your business set up.[7]

Isn't rent to rent very time-consuming? I don't want another job!

It depends on what you compare it with. If you compare rent to rent with a full-time job – working 40 hours, 40 weeks, 40 years – then no, it's not very time-consuming. In the beginning, it's going to take you a few hours a week but, once you get set up using our Rent 2 Rent Success System, it will only take you a few hours a month.

I see many people taking much longer than this to manage their properties because they haven't set things up with the end in mind; they ignore simple systems and processes that make life easy. Setting up your business according to a proven system will save your time, money and sanity! We'll talk more about how to get started with systems in Manage and Multiply. So many people struggle, when the unnecessary stress can be eliminated by implementing the simple systems we teach.

Now let's compare. Say you've got five rent to rent properties. Even with an average profit of £500 per month per property after bills and running costs, you've got a profit of £2,500 per month for a few hours' work each month. Compare that with an average UK salary (£24,500 in February 2020[8]) for which, if you're lucky, you work 40 hours a week – and maybe a lot more. Maybe your role is very stressful. Maybe you have to plead for holidays. Maybe you have a rough commute. Maybe you have a sinking feeling every Sunday evening.

Yes, you do have to put time into rent to rent to make it work, but it's a few hours a month in exchange for the freedom to live life on your terms. You do invest time, but the payoff is life-changing.

What if I can't fill the rooms and I'm tied in for three or five years?

It's a natural concern to have, and it's true that going into rent to rent without proper due diligence can create this problem. Within the Rent 2 Rent Success System, we explain exactly how to choose the right property in the right area and price it correctly for your target housemates. All this pre-work helps to ensure every deal works well in the long term.

Using the strategies I talk about in Manage and Multiply to rapidly fill your rooms has enabled us to keep voids (empty rooms) very low. Another strategy we use is to build in a rent-free period before the guaranteed rent starts. We know that at the start of the contract, it will take some time to tenant the property, so we agree a rent-free period with the landlord or agent. Additionally, we use the Rent 2 Rent Success Deal Analyser to forecast costs, allowing an amount for voids. This ensures that, even if you have some periods where you are between housemates, the property will still be profitable for you. These are just some of the things we do, with all parts of the system working together to produce a great result.

But let's say you were unaware of the processes for choosing the right property, analysing whether a property will work, and finding systems for keeping your rooms full. In this instance, if you decided you'd like to return the property, then you would speak with the landlord or agent to return the property by mutual agreement, or you would invoke the break clause in your contract. As we discussed earlier, it's important to have the right contract in place to allow for this, but I'll talk more about that in Make the Deals.

Follow a tried and tested system, like our Rent 2 Rent Success System. Although rent to rent is a simple concept, the implementation is nuanced, and mistakes can be very expensive.

Isn't the HMO market saturated?

Once you know something, it can feel like everyone and their dachshund knows the same thing. Now you are moving forward with your rent to rent business, you see HMOs everywhere. Yet the truth is that most people in the UK do not know what an HMO is, and they've never heard of rent to rent, although in the property world it can sometimes feel as though everyone is doing it. I start here because your perception may be skewed by your environment.

We know there is a shortfall in affordable housing. A National Housing Federation and Crisis report conducted by Heriot-Watt University revealed that the UK needs to build 340,000 new homes every year until 2031 to meet housing demand, and at least 145,000 of those homes need to be affordable.[9] In the 30 years between 1959 and 1988, 7.4 million houses were built in England; in the 30 years from 1989 to 2018, only 3.3 million were built. That's a shortfall of 3.1 million homes – over 104,000 homes a year – over the last 30 years.[10]

In 2018, the UK government estimated that there were around 4.5 million households living in about 497,000 HMOs in England and Wales.[11] Many councils have introduced planning changes, like Article 4, making it more difficult to create a new HMO. This means that the growth in HMOs is slowing. This reduces supply without decreasing demand, meaning there is actually more demand for HMOs than before.

Young professionals and contractors make up the majority of our housemates. Many of our housemates could easily afford to rent a one-bedroom flat but *prefer to share* as they love the convenience of having all their housing costs in one payment, with no utility bills, no broadband payment, and a home that's fully furnished and ready to roll.

Often the people claiming the HMO market is saturated have substandard properties in the wrong areas or don't have any HMOs at all, but they do have a lot of unsubstantiated opinions. We explain how to choose the properties that will rent consistently and how to ensure your properties are among the best available for the people you're targeting. This doesn't necessarily mean high-priced; you may choose to be among the best in the low- or mid-priced range for contractors, for example.

The HMO market is buoyant, not saturated.

Isn't it true that no one wants to live in shared houses after coronavirus?

This one seems like common sense. But it isn't, because people do still live in HMOs and continue to choose to move into HMOs. It's for the reasons I have mentioned and also:

, To meet people: often people are moving to a new city for work and don't know anyone. They actually prefer to live with other like-minded people rather than living alone.

, For affordability: often people are saving to buy their own home and love the affordability of HMOs because they can save more each month.

, For convenience: many people like the ease of moving in and having everything set up already, with furniture, all the bills included and fast service if anything goes wrong.

, For flexibility: many people move around the country with their roles, so it is easier for them to just commit for six months.

The demand has grown rather than diminished.

But rent to rent won't work in a recession!

Residential rental demand increases in recessions. More people prefer to rent rather than buy in an economic down-turn. In 2017, home ownership in England was at a 30-year low, according to the English Housing Survey, which found home ownership at its lowest level since 1985.[12] The private rental sector has doubled in size since 2004, with 4.5 million households, including almost 50% of people aged 25–34, renting their homes.

The Royal Institute of Chartered Surveyors shows that following the 2008 recession there was a continued rise in tenant demand.[13]

So, although many people state as fact that getting into rental in a recession is bad, they are wrong. Recessions see growing demand for rental property – and especially affordable rental property, such as HMOs.

Can I do rent to rent if I have bad credit?

You might be reading this thinking 'well, that's all very well in theory, but I don't think rent to rent is for me, because I have bad credit'. This is important, because with a low credit score it can be challenging to pass the referencing process with letting agents.

However, you can still do rent to rent if you have bad credit. Some of the most successful business people and entrepreneurs started off with nothing or were even significantly in debt. Many of them have gone bankrupt in the past. There are some provisos, so go through our 4 Step Credit Success Process to see if you're ready to get started in rent to rent right now. If you aren't, do those steps first and then get started afterwards.

> ▶ **Rockstar Essentials – Get our simple 4 Step Credit Success Process at rent2rentsuccess.com/essentials**

If you have bad credit, it's likely you've been through a challenging financial situation in the past. The resulting low score on your credit file is due to choices you made in the past that haven't turned out in the way you hoped.

 Everything happened exactly as it was supposed to.

I find it useful to believe that 'everything happened exactly as it was supposed to'. You were supposed to go through the challenging times you endured. You were supposed to overcome the obstacles you beat. You were supposed to grow stronger. You were supposed to grow wiser. You were supposed to move forward from exactly where you are today. So, forgive yourself – and others – for any past mistakes, and plan how to move forward successfully. I want you to believe that you will succeed in property.

When you start this process, your credit will improve over months, but it won't improve overnight. So, when you do start in rent to rent, I encourage you to work directly with landlords. Most landlords will not ask you for a credit report. You just need to make sure that your income and savings are such that you can afford to take on rent to rent. You need to have a good foundation and access to some money so that you can meet your obligations under the rent to rent agreement.

It's a fantastic way to start in business and to make positive changes in your life.

How could I make more money from a property than a professional letting agent or experienced landlord?

OK, so perhaps you can see that a landlord or letting agent might entrust you with a property. How could you make it worth more money so that you can pay a fair rent to the land-lord *and* charge a fair rent to tenants?

Earlier I explained that, of the three ways to do rent to rent, HMOs give the highest return on money and time invested, especially for beginners. It's easy to see how you can make more money renting a property out by the room rather than offering the property as a single let.

Yet I suggested that you choose *existing* HMOs. That means the properties are already being let out by the room, which prompts people to wonder how they can achieve higher rents than the landlords or letting agent previously did. When a property is already an HMO, you'd assume the owner or let-ting agent is already used to higher rents, but this isn't always the case.

The way we are able to achieve higher rents is by using our HMO systems, which many landlords and agents are unaware of, or do not implement. We complete a light refurbishment of the property (sometimes we pay, sometimes the owner pays). We dress the rooms attractively and we provide good service. It's the last one that provides the most uplift.

What it means is that we can take HMOs that are not performing as well as they could be and achieve higher rents consistently, as we show in Model Magic.

But surely rent to rent doesn't work in Article 4 areas?

'Article 4' is a direction under Article 4 of the General Permitted Development Order that enables councils to remove some 'permitted development rights'. Article 4 requires a planning application to be submitted to the relevant council in order to change a house to an HMO.

Many people who've made the assumption that rent to rent only works if you convert a single let to a house share believe existing HMOs won't work. *You* now know, though, that rent to rent works on existing HMOs. Therefore, you can operate in *all* areas, even Article 4 areas. But sh, don't tell everyone – let's keep it between ourselves!

What about those news stories about loads of people being crammed into a tiny house and paying very high rents?

You're reading this book because you definitely do not want to be associated with anything that is disreputable or causes harm. You are in the right place. We show you how to create beautiful affordable homes people love to live in. Working ethically to add value for both tenants and landlords is the foundation of everything we do.

Recently, a local letting agent referred a drama school to us. The drama school has young students joining from all over the world, usually female and usually living away from home for the first time. The letting agent knew the drama school wanted to be sure its students would be well cared for, so they thought of us. We put care into selecting new house-mates who are a good fit with existing tenants, and we go way beyond minimum standards in terms of the homes and the service we provide, as shown in over 70 five-star Google reviews from housemates and landlords. In the Rent 2 Rent Success System, we show you how to provide a great service *in little time* and have a business you're proud of. It's a process to have an amazing business without it taking over your life and becoming another job.

Yes, there are rogue landlords, as there are rogue businesses in every industry. Sensationalist TV programming can create the feeling that these landlords are the majority, rather than a tiny minority.

It does irk me that so often the rogue operators dominate the conversation when it comes to rent to rent. It's another reason I'm so passionate about sharing with you the ethical way to do rent to rent. The more of us who can provide beautiful homes of the type we'd be happy to rent to our family, the quicker the charlatans will be ousted from the industry. We'll build a community of ethical providers who care.

I'll show you some examples of our properties in Model Magic.

Hmm. Isn't this ripping off landlords who'd get more rent without you?

Often, we are able to pay landlords *more* than they were receiving before in net rent. By 'net rent', I mean the rent a landlord receives after the cost of council tax, gas, electricity, water, Wi-Fi, minor maintenance, cleaning, gardening, and voids (times when rooms are empty, which have a cost too). Most landlords know what the gross rent received from the tenant is, but are unsure of their net income.

When we take on a property, we pay these costs. Working with us can actually provide landlords with more income than they were receiving when their property was managed by a high street letting agent, simply because we're able to manage HMOs more diligently and are HMO specialists, whereas a typical letting agent will manage hundreds of properties and specialise in single lets rather than HMOs.

Ironically, many of the landlords we work with have been badly let down by traditional letting agents. For example, Robbie had two HMOs that were managed by letting agents for over 12 years, but they had descended into a state of terrible disrepair before he found us. I'll share more on Robbie's story in Model Magic.

We adopt an ethical approach. The Rent 2 Rent Success System creates a win-win-win:

, A win for the property owner: guaranteed rent, freedom from tenant management and total peace of mind.

, A win for your housemates: beautiful, affordable homes they love to live in.

, A win for you: the consistent cashflow you need to live life on your terms.

Maybe you're thinking 'I understand how rent to rent works, but it's not for me because I want to buy properties'. Let's talk about that.

Rent to rent is a cashflow business. What if I want to buy properties and leave a legacy for my family or causes I care about?

Some people are put off rent to rent because it's a cashflow business; you don't own the properties. And most of us want to own property too, to take advantage of capital appreciation and be able to pass assets on to our children and others who are important to us.

Not only can rent to rent help you make a great living from properties you don't own, it can help you build your own property portfolio using creative strategies like lease options and exchange with delayed completion. This means you can buy properties without having £50k in the bank.

Lease options and exchange with delayed completion are strategies where you buy properties without a mortgage or big deposit up front. They're sometimes known as 'no money down' strategies because you can secure properties for as little as £1 instead of needing a big deposit. The basic principle is that you agree a price with the owner that you will pay in the future. These deals can be agreed in many different ways; we give you an example in Model Magic.

If you're not yet in a position to buy your own investment properties – or if you already own buy-to-lets and you've run out of money – rent to rent is a great way to build your cashflow and your credibility before you move on to growing your long-term wealth by buying your own assets. You'll find you can use creative strategies, such as the ones we've talked about here. It'll also be much easier to attract private investors and traditional bank lending once you have a track record in property with your rent to rent business.

Rent to rent won't work for me because I am too young/am too old/have children/am too shy/have a strong accent

You are enough! I remind you of this because I see in our Kickstarter Programme that most of us have so much self-doubt, irrespective of how many achievements we have. So, if you're reading this and thinking 'I couldn't do that because', then I want to remind you of something:

- You are not too young.
- You are not too old.
- You don't have too many children.
- You are not too shy.
- Your accent is not too strong.

I can say this confidently because these are all concerns people have expressed to me before they successfully got their first deal. There are people right now who have success in rent to rent who:

- Are younger than you
- Are older than you
- Have more children than you
- Are shyer than you
- Have a stronger accent than you.

You are enough exactly as you are. And you will succeed. Will you be amazing straight out of the gate? Probably not. But the good news is:

'You don't have to be great to get started, but you do have to get started to be great.'

— Zig Ziglar

Just get started. Most of us give up on ourselves before we've started; I did that and wasted too many years. And we waste time listening to people who don't have the results we're looking for. People who don't have the answers we need. People who have never invested in property, never had a business. People who complain about their lives. If there's one lesson I wish I'd understood earlier, it's that you should listen to those who have done what you'd like to do. They understand how to move past the obstacles you need to navigate. They can show you short cuts to success.

Don't just blindly accept what anyone – including me – says to you. Take all new information and ask the ultimate authority, the one who has your best interests at heart, the one who knows you inside out. Ask *you*!

Let's dive in now. I'd like to introduce you to the Rent 2 Rent Success System.

PART 2

HOW TO BECOME A

RENT 2 RENT

ROCKSTAR

DISCOVER THE RENT 2 RENT
SUCCESS SYSTEM

Rock the stage in your own life.

"IF THEY DON'T GIVE YOU A SEAT AT THE TABLE, BRING A FOLDING CHAIR."

Shirley Chisholm

INTRODUCTION TO THE RENT 2 RENT SUCCESS SYSTEM

'Why not you? Why not now?'

— Jim Rohn

You may be at the very beginning of your journey. Here in Part 2, I show you the structure of our six-step Rent 2 Rent Success System. Nicky and I wanted to give you as much as we possibly could in this book, so we chose to include the full overview rather than just the first few steps. This will be incredibly helpful for you when you are ready to get started.

We have poured as much as we can into the limited space in a book. Of course, it's impossible to fit *everything* you need to run a successful business into one book, but our goal was to give you the complete six-step system and actionable steps you can take. We've also created a **Rockstar Essentials** hub with more resources you can use and exercises you can do; these will help you get even better results from the book. You can access them at **rent2rentsuccess.com/essentials**

We've talked about the fact there are a lot of myths about rent to rent. Lots of people will tell you it's not possible. However, you also know there are many people doing rent to rent ethically and successfully. They are providing a great service, making money from properties they don't own and living life on their terms.

WHAT IS THE RENT 2 RENT SUCCESS SYSTEM?

The Rent 2 Rent Success System is a roadmap for ethical rent to rent success. It provides six steps to achieve success quickly, and in a way where everyone wins. You'll feel invigorated and uplifted as you move towards your goals. What took us years to learn and improve, you can implement in days and weeks. We love sharing this so much that I'm always surprised when I recall how much we resisted teaching it!

WHY WE DECIDED TO SHARE OUR RENT 2 RENT SUCCESS SYSTEM

When HMO Heaven began to take off, people asked us constantly, 'How are you doing this?', 'How do I get started?', 'Why would a landlord give a property to me?', 'How do I know this is a good deal?' and lots more. We made videos and sent long replies to lots of emails. We referred people to other training courses, yet they came back asking for more detail and for more information about how to implement it, or for templates to help them to make offers, or for checklists on how to onboard housemates. They wanted *our way*. People wanted to know how *we* did it.

At first, we were reluctant. You see, in the property industry, trainers are often seen as selling snake oil, 'selling a dream', and that was not what we wanted to do. That is why, for quite a while, we stuck to our stance not to do paid training. That only changed when Janet (not her real name), who'd paid thousands for property training, came back to me to say that she didn't understand what to do next. I asked, of course, if she had asked her trainer for help. Janet told me that the fee she had paid was for in-person training, but after that… nothing. In theory, there was a Facebook group, but in practice the trainers didn't help very much. Now that Janet was actioning the information, she needed their help to understand whether she was doing things correctly and what she should do next, in specific situations unique to her.

I was shocked when Janet showed me the course materials. It was clear these documents were not being used within the trainer's business. I could see the level of detail was not there – everything was at a very superficial level. It looked as though the trainer had just whipped up a few flimsy Word documents for the course. There was no step by step process taking someone from the idea of starting in rent to rent right through to creating consistent cashflow. It was very much down to Janet to work out what to do next – on her own. When she signed up, she thought she'd get everything she needed; what she really got was a fantastic training event at a hotel with lots of energy and enthusiasm, but there was no substance behind it. After she'd left the hotel, that was it. Nothing. She was on her own – unless she took the upsell for well over five figures more on another course.

It was easy to see why people lose faith in property trainers. And I immediately thought, 'We could do this much better simply by adding care.' It reminded me of the moment I talked about earlier, when I listened to a speaker and was inspired to do rent to rent itself in a different way. I felt confident we could provide better training, because so many people were doing it without any care. They showed no concern over whether people were successful or not. We knew we could help others succeed and felt duty-bound to share what we had found out late in life: the ethical way to make money from property without buying it, and the freedom it gives you to live life on your terms.

It felt right. We would include all the things we use within our business to be successful, and we would provide a full step by step system for success. We would be there for people as they implemented the system, and we would provide encouragement, inspiration and information over the longer term. And, importantly, we would provide the foundations for systemising your business so that running it gives you freedom.

Nicky and I were very clear, though, that we wanted to work with people who cared about doing a good job, not people who just wanted to 'get rich quick'. We wanted to show people the ethical way to succeed, and we wanted to actually see them succeed by providing the ongoing support they needed as they moved forward. We didn't want to offer a one-, two- or three-day course with no follow-up. Our Kickstarter Programme is step by step, with weekly support and accountability and daily help. The following chapters outline the same six-step system we go through in our programme. Our approach has been incredibly successful for students we've worked with, some of whom you'll meet in this book.

It was clear from the conversations I was having that people also wanted to be in a supportive environment that would keep them accountable and motivated. We decided to build a community of ethical people who would be offering a good service and doing things properly. Our incredible Kickstarter Community of supportive, ambitious, inspiring people who have committed to success is one of the aspects of the programme that we get the most positive feedback about. It's one of the reasons why our Kickstarter students have had so many life-changing results.

And I also wanted to emphasise that even a very small number of properties can be life-changing. I wanted to give something to people like me, who felt they didn't have the right connections, the right experience, or enough money to get started and be successful.

That was what eventually led to our Rent 2 Rent Success System being born. We've taken what we've learned over the

"

Even a very small
number of properties
can be life-changing.

years and created a step by step system to help professionals to quickly get started in property.

It's for people who are ready for a change, who want the freedom that consistent cashflow would bring them, people who have the spark for more. The money is important, of course, but I know from speaking to people that it's the freedom they value most. Mark Fitzgerald, who was part of our very first Kickstarter Programme, found it was life-changing for him.

MARK FITZGERALD'S STORY

It [rent to rent] has given me more freedom and more time. You know, the biggest thing for me in the last 12 months has been the fact that I've been able to go to my sons' sports days. I've been able to go to their parents' evenings. If they're not very well, we are not struggling for somebody to go and pick them up from school. I can do it. It's great just being there for my kids. My eldest is 14 and I missed all of that. It's time you can't get back.

In this book, we're going to guide you through the six-step Rent 2 Rent Success System. The advantage of following the system is that you have the fast track to success. There's such a benefit in knowing you are following a proven system rather than having to make all the time-consuming and costly mistakes yourself.

Here's how the Rent 2 Rent Success System works:

Rent 2 Rent Success

1. Model Magic

Understand the real magic in the rent to rent model, how it works, how it has worked for others, and how it can work for you.

2. Mindset Mastery

Discover the powerful tools to go from sometime procrastinator to consistent action-taker. Get ready to fly!

3. Mind Your Business

Start your business quickly, legally and inexpensively, even if you have no business or property experience.

4. Magnetic Marketing

Attract owners and agents to you with our unique Magnetic Marketing methods, which work even if you hate selling or are shy.

5. Make the Deals

Discover how to analyse deals in minutes, negotiate like a ninja and do the deals!

6. Manage and Multiply

Understand how to manage and systemise your business, for the freedom you want as your business grows.

This is your path to consistent cashflow and the freedom to live a life you truly love.

6

MULTIPLY

4 MAGNETIC MARKETING

5 MAKE THE DEALS

1 MODEL MAGIC

2 MINDSET MASTERY

3 MIND YOUR BUSINESS

The Rent to Rent Success System

STEP

1

MODEL MAGIC

Understand the real magic in the rent to rent model, how it works, how it has worked for others, and how it can work for you.

'Don't ask for permission, give notice.'

Lisa Nichols

WHAT IS MODEL MAGIC?

This first step is about ensuring we build on solid foundations. Getting these basics right first will give you ease and grace in making consistent cashflow from properties you don't own and having the freedom to live life on your own terms. Ethically.

WHY IS MODEL MAGIC IMPORTANT TO RENT 2 RENT SUCCESS?

This is the practical foundational knowledge, which means the difference between peace and profitability, and frustration and failure. This part is a little bit denser, but I encourage you to stay with it and understand these basics, because they are critical to your success.

For every step, there are short cuts and time savers, ways to do things right and ways to do things wrong. These now seem like common sense to me, but so many people get into hot water because they think that because the concept of rent to rent is simple, there is no best practice. Don't underestimate the power of knowing how to get things right – the first time. It will save you so much time, money and stress.

HOW TO CREATE MODEL MAGIC

In this chapter, you'll learn:

1. **How to choose your area – the 4 Ps.**
2. **What you need to know about HMO licensing.**
3. **What makes a good HMO – the 4 Ls.**
4. **How our ethical win-win-win approach works – real life case studies.**
5. **How rent to rent can help you buy properties without a big deposit.**

HOW TO CHOOSE YOUR AREA – THE 4 Ps

If you feel very confused about where to start, this section will give you clarity. Rent to rent works in most cities; there are people doing it all over the country. Of course, there are checks to make first. And that's what I'll talk to you about now, to make sure it's going to be a good area for you.

We've developed the 4 Ps to help you assess whether an area will work well.

Practical – start where you are!

Choose an area you know well as your first location. People overlook how much easier this will make the process. Choosing somewhere close to your home or workplace will give you so much more clarity than trying to get your very first property far away in an area unknown to you. That's not impossible, but it's much more difficult – and we like to make things as simple as possible. As you don't need to buy the property, you can do this even if you live in an expensive area like London.

It needs to be close to you because, if you're doing the setup and getting the property together at the beginning, it'll run much more smoothly when you can get to it easily. Later on, you may choose to outsource (as we did), but until then, it's best that you make sure it works for you. All of our properties are within 20 minutes' drive of where we live, although we have now outsourced our property management to an in-house assistant property manager. 'Near' is a relative term and depends on you. If you do a lot of driving, one hour away might feel close enough. Work out what works for you and stick to it for your first property.

Then you'll need to look at a few other things, just to make sure that the location is really going to work well from an HMO perspective.

People hubs – be where the people are going!

Your property should also be near people hubs. These are things like:

, Hospitals
, Large employers
, Universities
, Shops, cafes and restaurants.

People hubs are the reasons people are coming to your city. The more people hubs there are in your location, the more resilient it is as an investment area.

Public transport links – be easy to get to!

Around 50% of our housemates drive, which is a high percentage for HMO housemates; in many areas, most won't drive. Good transport links nearby are important, and it's even more important if you're in an area where fewer of your housemates drive.

Property type in your area – be where the HMOs are!

You want to check that there are HMOs in the area. You want to see signs of development and investment as well. If the area you're focusing on doesn't have many large properties and is mainly two-bed houses or flats, it's not going to work.

Once you know your location has the essential 4 Ps, you'll want to see whether the demand is there.

Demand

SpareRoom

SpareRoom.com is currently the number one website for letting shared houses in the UK, by a country mile. It will show you the number of people looking for rooms, the number of rooms available, the rents and the conditions of the properties. You'll be able to see rooms from the lowest to the highest end of the market so you can assess where you want to position yourself.

SpareRoom will give you an *indication* of demand. Remember not every available room will be listed and not every listed room will be available. Equally, not every potential housemate looking for a property will have created an account on Spare-Room. But you'll be able to find out the ratio of people looking for rooms versus the rooms available. Obviously, an area becomes more appealing when the number of people looking for rooms far exceeds the number of rooms available. Our area works well, yet the ratio of potential housemates looking versus the rooms available on SpareRoom varies massively at different times of the year, so you need to consider other factors too. As I write this, there are approximately the same number of rooms available in our area as people looking for rooms; that would suggest this is not a good area, although we know it is. So, I just urge you to take SpareRoom findings as an indication and not a definitive answer.

Your local knowledge

This is where your knowledge of the area helps you massively, as you'll have an idea whether your area is attracting lots of new people or not, and the rentability of different locations listed on SpareRoom. Don't underplay your local knowledge. You know your area!

Local agents and investors

You can also speak to local letting agents and landlords, although I caution you not to put too much weight on what they say if they're not HMO specialists. Lots of HMO investors contact us about investing in Newport and tell us that local high street letting agents in our area have advised them that HMOs don't work where we are based! All it means is that HMOs don't work for some high street letting agents because it's not their specialism and they prefer single lets.

With your location decided, you will be able to drive forward with creating your business and making your aspirations a reality. This is a critical first step; let's do it together.

WHAT YOU NEED TO KNOW ABOUT HMO LICENSING

Many people I talk to are intimidated by licensing. Licensing looks complicated but once you understand the basics, it's straightforward. Remember that lots of people are doing it and most of them aren't rocket scientists. You'll be able to do it too, and the fact that some people are put off by HMO licensing means there will be more opportunity for you!

What is HMO licensing?

HMO licensing relates to the rules the government states must be followed for an HMO.

Mandatory licensing rules in England and Wales

Every HMO property for five or more people from more than one household requires an HMO licence. It used to only apply to properties with more than two storeys, but now it is the case for all HMOs, irrespective of the number of floors. Properties for seven or more people from two or more households require *sui generis* HMO planning.[14]

Mandatory licensing rules in Scotland

Slightly different rules apply in Scotland; you will need an HMO licence if you want to rent your HMO property out to three or more tenants, when none of them are related or part of the same household.[15]

Local differences

Some councils have added further specifics to the national requirements, so you'll need to find out whether there are any additional restrictions in the areas you're looking at. The additional requirements can be in the form of Article 4 direction or additional or selective licensing.

Let me explain what this means.

Article 4 direction

This is a direction under **Article 4 of the General Permitted Development Order,** which enables the Secretary of State or local planning authorities to withdraw specified permitted property development rights. What Article 4 means in plain English is that a planning application has to be submitted to the relevant council to change a house to an HMO, even for three or four people, which under the national legislation wouldn't require planning. (It should be noted that planning permission is, and always has been, required to convert a single family house into a large HMO with seven or more unrelated persons sharing.)

Additional licensing

This applies to certain HMOs that fall outside the scope of the mandatory HMO licensing scheme. It's a discretionary scheme that a council may have adopted to help it deal with the issues associated with HMOs that are not already covered by mandatory licensing.

Selective licensing

As with additional licensing, the content will depend on exactly how the council has drafted its scheme. Some schemes cover the whole borough, whereas others only apply to smaller geographical areas.

EXERCISE

Choose Your Location

Remember that rent to rent works in cities across the country. You just need to pick one, so which location are you going to choose?

Use our 4 Ps and the easy-to-complete worksheet to make the best choice for you.

Download our **Choose Your Location Worksheet** now from **rent2rentsuccess.com/essentials** and let's get started.

1st P: Practical – start where you are!

▶ *Action*

Add some locations to the table. They should be close to where you live or work. Remember: you are renting a property, not buying it, so you don't need to exclude expensive areas.

Next, for each of your chosen locations, consider the following. Add additional columns if your target housemate type has a particular need or requirement (e.g. proximity to an airport if you want to target airline crews).

2nd P: People hubs – be where the people are going!

▶ *Action*

Tick the people hubs that apply. The more people hubs you tick, the more attractive your property will likely be to your prospective housemates. That would obviously mean your rooms will be rented quickly and will stay rented, too.

3rd P: Public transport links – be easy to get to!

▶ *Action*

Tick whether there are good transport links to your property, and from your property to other people hubs. In many areas, most HMO housemates won't drive. If you think a high percentage of your target housemates will drive, consider whether there is good parking rather than just transport links.

4th P: Property type in your area – be where the HMOs are!

▶ *Action*

Tick if there are already HMOs and large properties in the area, and signs of development and investment.

Demand

▶ *Action*

Tick if there is demand in the area. Look at SpareRoom, use your own local knowledge of the area, and check in with local agents and investors.

Licensing

▶ *Action*

Tick what licensing applies to the area.

Well done! With the table completed, it will be easier to make an informed decision about which location to choose.

▶ *Action*

Assess the table you have completed and choose your location!

TOP TIP

How do I know whether there is Article 4 or additional/selective licensing in my area?

This is very simple. The information is publicly available on the council website of each area.

My area is covered by Article 4. What should I do?

As we discussed in Mythbusters, Article 4 areas work especially well for rent to rent. We have a successful rent to rent business in an Article 4 equivalent area; because we focus on existing HMOs, it doesn't stop us.

 Article 4 gives you an advantage, because over time the number of HMOs decreases while tenant demand remains the same, making it even easier to rent your rooms.

When you focus on existing HMOs, everything is already done for you. You don't need to pay for additional works. You don't have the uncertainty about whether planning will be granted. And yes, landlords and agents will rent existing HMOs to you on a rent to rent basis. We talk more about that in Magnetic Marketing.

Sometimes, it can be worth the time and expense of going through planning; for example, if you're buying a property or if you have the property on a very long lease at a no-brainer rent. Generally, though, we do not recommend that beginners go for properties that aren't existing HMOs in Article 4 areas – although there are exceptions to every rule. Rent 2 Rent Rockstar Maria Opaniran took this approach, and her council said hers was one of the best HMOs they'd seen. You can hear her tell the story in her own words on our website[16].

That's licensing sorted. Let's move on to what makes a good HMO.

WHAT MAKES A GOOD HMO – THE 4 Ls

The things you learn here will set you up for consistent cashflow and the freedom you want. This is an area where many people without support come unstuck because they are confused about whether a particular property will work well for rent to rent.

Having been through this process so many times, we've created our own system for assessing whether properties will work well for rent to rent. There are 4 Ls to look out for:

1st L: Licensing

We've talked about HMO licensing already. Remember: we suggest that, to start off with, you select properties that already have an HMO licence.

2nd L: Location

We discussed choosing a location with lots of people hubs nearby and plenty of demand. For professional tenants, good transport links, local shops and bars and restaurants are also a plus. For contractors, we've found that parking is more important than local amenities, as they often work long hours and are just there to work, not to socialise. The location you choose needs to be a location where your target housemates would want to live.

3rd L: Layout

The next L is layout, and this is important. What I mean by layout is assessing whether the house will be pleasant to live in as a house share. Our ethical approach takes us beyond what the legal requirements are. It's more of a 'Would I be happy for my niece or nephew to live here?'

It needs to have a good-sized living space – but what counts as 'good-sized' can vary around the country. In some parts of London, for example, you don't need a separate lounge to be able to rent out your property consistently; people are very happy with a larger and more social kitchen. Do look at what works well for people in your area, and consider what creates a living environment you can feel proud of.

Where a two-bed house has been chopped up to create a five-bed, two-bath HMO, often those buildings just don't work well as places for five people to live in, unless they've been substantially extended. Think about that, because it will impact you. You need to ensure that the property you choose is a lovely place to live, and that the living area and bedrooms feel well sized. I don't just mean 'above minimum size'. I mean they feel like a good place to live. A house needs to flow. It needs to feel like a lovely home for a group of people.

"

We want to create

a home people love

coming home to.

"

4th L: Lifestyle

Our final L is lifestyle. It's up to us to ensure we are creating a lifestyle that people want. We want to create a home people love coming home to. And our role as HMO landlords is to make that home as good as it can be, to attract the right potential housemates.

One of the things we notice that people really love is extra space. They love *extra storage*. While you can't change the size of a house without major works, you can increase the storage and make it feel more spacious at the same time.

TOP TIP

We've found having two wardrobes can be a real winner. Look at how you can add storage space; when you do it thoughtfully, you're giving people a better lifestyle and experience.

Now that people are more likely to be working from home than in the past, a desk and attractive work area and fast broadband are also important. Ensure there are enough kitchen units; fridge and freezer space is important, too. In some properties, we added extra kitchen units. This goes well at viewings, because people can see that we really care and have thought about the little practical things that make a huge difference day to day.

People love en suites. If you have them, your properties will be more in demand than if you don't. Having said that, most of our properties have shared bathrooms and still rent consistently. The fewer people sharing a bathroom, the more attractive a property becomes to potential housemates. We find that three people sharing a bathroom is an absolute maximum. A typical house share with five people and two bathrooms has a ratio of two and a half people per bathroom. Two people sharing is better, but en suites are the crème de la crème.

Around 50% of our tenants drive a car and, for them, parking is really important. When we're selling those rooms, one out of every two viewers will be a driver, so having some properties with parking, whether on-street or dedicated spaces, will be attractive.

Of course, these are guidelines. In many parts of London, parking is the exception rather than the norm and so it isn't expected. However, it's almost always the case that if parking is easily available outside the property, the HMO will be more attractive to more people than if it isn't.

The sooner you get all that right, the fewer voids you have, the happier your housemates, and the more profitable your business will be. If the HMO is in the right location, next to lots of people hubs, and it has a great layout and space feel, it will create a good lifestyle for the people who live there.

REAL LIFE CASE STUDIES SHOWING OUR WIN-WIN-WIN ETHICAL APPROACH

Let's bring this to life with a case study. You might think you need property experience to be successful in rent to rent, and you might think it's what landlords and agents are looking for, so they would rule you out. However, the case study shows that isn't the case at all, and it also shows how everyone wins: our landlords, our housemates, and us.

Our story

This is the story of our first deal. It happened before we felt ready, and it happened *without* HMO experience.

Photo: Our first property - secured!

Here we are at the front door of our very first property. I was still working full-time as a contractor in financial services. I was half excited, confident and enjoying the thrill of this new path, and half terrified I was making a hideous mistake and would end up wishing I'd listened to all the people who'd told me it wouldn't work. At first, the very idea someone would entrust their property to me was laughable, but I leaned into it because I felt so determined. Mum's telephone call continually came back to haunt me.

Actually, it wasn't so much the call itself. It was reflecting on it that afternoon in the bank – on that feeling, that awful feeling in my gut as I knew I'd made the wrong decision. The moment I realised I was making the bank and the job more important than the people I loved and cared for, the people I said were important to me. My actions didn't show what I wanted my priorities to be. Whenever I thought of giving up, feeling these feelings spurred me on.

These feelings were what spurred me to walk into a large high street letting agent one Saturday lunchtime. I hovered a safe distance away. Out of sight (I hoped!). Dithering. Shifting my weight from one leg to the other. Talking myself into and out of and into and out of and…

Eventually, I had a word with myself. 'Stephanie, pull yourself together and go on in. What's the worst that could happen?' And I went in.

'Do you have any HMOs?' I heard myself saying in a strangled-sounding voice that didn't sound like me at all.

'Hmm, is it subletting? We don't do subletting.'

'Oh, I see… maybe that's something for the smaller independent agents we work with…' (Where was I getting this stuff from?)

'Head Office would need to approve, and I don't think it would get approval for the contracts.'

'Right. Well, I suppose with you not knowing us, you'd want to get to know our work first before vouching for us to Head Office. Would you consider introducing us to any of your 'tenant find only' landlords?' (I'm really amazed with myself here; this was not something I'd planned.)

Suddenly, it was as though a lightbulb had gone off in her head, and she started ushering me across to a large screen. There she brought up two listings for HMOs on the same street, just a few doors away from each other.

'Oh my goodness,' I thought, 'what if we get this deal?' (Excitement!)

'Oh my goodness,' I thought, 'what if we get this deal?' (Terror!)

How I kept my composure, I really don't know – but I did. And we arranged a viewing.

At the viewing, Nicky and I met the owner and the letting agent. My heart was racing as we walked around the house. We could see that the locations were great and these were houses that people would love to live in. We felt the landlord was a good man, too, who cared about his tenants – that is so important.

So, how did we get our first deal when we had no experience? Because landlords and letting agents are looking for something more important than experience; the number one thing they want is someone they can trust. When our very first landlord met us, he wasn't sure whether we'd last. Years later, he told us we had seemed a little green. We were! But he was a good judge of character who trusted our intentions and decided to take a chance on us. He could see our enthusiasm and quiet commitment. He could see how much we wanted to do well. And he could see how much focus we'd put on his properties, our only properties: 100%. This was in contrast to most high street letting agents, where he'd be one of hundreds. He also liked that it was guaranteed rent, so he knew what he'd be receiving each month, come what may.

Our first properties were a four-bed and a five-bed HMO, each advertised for £800 a month, and we got them for just £600 per month. That might seem unbelievably low if you're in London. The back story is that they had been £1,100 and £1,000 per month, but then student lets died when the local university closed its Newport campus. The landlord was not as interested in the amount of rent as he was in the security and hassle-free aspect we could offer. He'd been a landlord for well over 30 years and he'd seen it all in that time.

We ended up spending an absolute fortune on the refurbishment, though. Most of our Kickstarters now spend up to

£3,000 on a refurb; somehow, due to rookie errors, we spent £12,000! We now know all the things *not* to do, and we'll share that with you in Manage and Multiply. When we'd completed the refurb, we were excited and delighted. We absolutely loved what we'd created. The landlord was so amazed, he invited his elderly parents to view it. They knew the properties well, as for many years they'd helped to clean them during the annual student turnover time.

Now, when I look back, I do cringe at some of the styling! I thought I was an interior designer, but I'm definitely not. We now understand the simple way to dress a room inexpensively and effectively.

Photo: Before Refurbishment

Photo: After Refurbishment

The numbers:

INCOME	
RENT IN FROM TENANTS, ALLOWING FOR VOIDS	£1,921

OUTGOING	
GUARANTEED RENT TO OWNER	£600
TOTAL BILLS INCLUDING COUNCIL TAX, TV LICENCE & WI-FI	£505
INSURANCE (CONTENTS), MAINTENANCE, CLEANING & GARDENING	

REFURBISHMENT, FURNITURE & DRESSING	
TOTAL INVESTMENT WAS £12,594.00, SPREAD OVER FIVE-YEAR TERM	£211.06

CASHFLOW AFTER DEDUCTING ALL COSTS ABOVE	
MONTHLY	£605
ANNUALLY	£7,260
EVERY FIVE YEARS	£36,300

And the great thing is that, in spite of our rookie mistakes and spending too much on the refurb, we still made over £600 each month, including the refurb costs. Then the landlord signed up with us for another five years, so we'll manage his properties for eight years in total. On this one, it's a cashflow of £56,685 over eight years, even taking into account all costs (including voids).

In Mythbusters, we touched on how we are able to make more money from each property without 'ripping off' either landlords or tenants, and I want to explain more how that is possible.

The reason we are able to do this is by *adding* value, not by taking away what is already there. In many cases, the properties are not managed well beforehand, so they have empty rooms.

ROBBIE'S STORY

In our fourth property, the landlord I mentioned earlier, Robbie, had been badly let down by a traditional high street letting agent. He lived hours away and relied upon his agents to manage the properties. At the time, he was losing hundreds of pounds every month. He was shocked by what he found at his properties and was pleased to try our services even though we were relatively new because, he said, even if we delivered half of what we promised, he'd be delighted.

'I'm delighted – from the state of near destruction [my property was in before], through the refurbishment to the introduction of quality tenants and the ongoing management, HMO Heaven has been exceptional. Meeting and working with HMO Heaven has been a life-changer.'

We don't take anything away from landlords or tenants; we create value where it didn't exist. Because we manage the properties well, the rental income goes up, so we're able to pay more to Robbie while still charging an affordable rent to housemates and making a profit ourselves.

Photo: Before Refurbishment

Photo: After Refurbishment

HOW RENT TO RENT CAN HELP YOU BUY PROPERTIES WITHOUT A BIG DEPOSIT

Finally, I'd like to discuss something people often overlook: rent to rent can help you *buy* property, too! And without a huge deposit or a mortgage.

Some people are put off rent to rent because it's a property business rather than a property investment, as you don't own the properties. However, rent to rent can be a wonderful first step to buying investment properties. There are creative strategies that allow you to buy properties without a big deposit or a mortgage, as we've touched on before. The main ones are lease options and exchange with delayed completion. The main

Photo: Our exchange with delayed completion property

difference is that with a lease option you have the *option* to buy a property by an agreed date for an agreed price, whereas in an exchange with delayed completion you have the *obligation* to buy a property by an agreed date for an agreed price.

The idea that a property owner would want to sell their property and receive the money over time instead of all at once is confusing to most people, but it happens more often than you might think, for lots of different reasons. Let me give you an example of how one of our agreements works.

OUR STORY – BUYING A PROPERTY EXCHANGE WITH DELAYED COMPLETION

Here are the numbers, which I will explain below:

AGREED COMPLETION DATE	WITHIN 5 YEARS
AGREED PURCHASE PRICE	£160,000
OPTION FEE, PAYABLE TO SELLER:	£16,000
MONTHLY PAYMENT, PAYABLE TO SELLER	£320
BALANCE AFTER 5 YEARS, PAYABLE TO SELLER: (£160K-£16K-(£320 X 60 MONTHS)	£124,800
MONTHLY CASHFLOW*	£1,426
ANNUAL CASHFLOW*	£17,112
5 YEARS CASHFLOW*	£85,560

(after paying Monthly payment payable to owner & operating expenses)

What we've agreed in this case is that we'll buy the property over time. So, we don't need a 30% deposit (£48,000 up front) and we won't need a mortgage right now.

We paid a one-off option fee payment of £16,000. (You can do these types of deals where you pay as little as £1 upfront;

that's why they're sometimes called 'no money down' deals. The option fee can be whatever is agreeable to both buyer and seller.) We then make a monthly payment of £320. These sums of £320 each month are deducted from the balance we will pay for the property in five years' time. Essentially, this means it's rent-free.

At the purchase date, which must be within five years, we will then deduct the £16,000 option fee and the monthly payments from the purchase price of £160,000. If we buy in five years' time, the balance to pay will be £124,800, which we can pay using a mortgage, private finance, or our own funds saved from the cashflow achieved from this and other properties.

If we hadn't been in rent to rent, we wouldn't have seen this opportunity, or the other properties we're buying using creative strategies. And these are opportunities that will come your way once you're doing rent to rent and talking to landlords and letting agents. You can hear Kickstarter Maria Opaniran talking about her lease option on her very first property on the **Rockstar Essentials** site[17].

It's important to be part of a community that normalises the result you're trying to achieve. Most of us have heard the phrase 'you're the average of the people you spend the most time with'. Can you imagine talking to friends and family who aren't savvy about creative property strategies about buying properties without a big deposit or mortgage? That's why people in our Rent 2 Rent Kickstarter Community value it so highly; it offers the support of other ambitious people on the same path to sit alongside the step by step guidance we provide.

SUMMARY OF MODEL MAGIC

In this chapter, we discussed:

- The 4 Ps of how to choose your area: ensuring that it's Practical, near People hubs and Public transport links, and that it has the right Property types, then assessing demand
- HMO licensing and why Article 4 is a blessing rather than a curse
- The 4 Ls of how to choose a property: Licensing, Location, Layout and Lifestyle
- Real life case studies showing the ethical win-win-win approach
- How rent to rent can help you buy properties.

I hope this leaves you energised and excited, rather than overwhelmed. Sometimes we see people get overwhelmed thinking about managing twenty properties when they have none, and this stops them moving forward. If that's you, now is a good time to remind you of a key point.

 Your focus is: one. You only need one property to get started. Focus all your energies on your very next step.

Our first two properties brought cashflow of over £1,000 per month, *after* all the running costs. What would *you* do with an extra £12,000 each year... £60,000 every five years?

Many of us have had plans before and not succeeded in moving forward. In the next chapter, I explain what to do when you are your own worst enemy.

Writing your Rent 2 Rent Success Story will be much easier with the insights of Mindset Mastery. Let's dive in!

STEP 2
MINDSET MASTERY

Discover the powerful tools to go from sometime procrastinator to consistent action-taker. Get ready to fly!

'Are you creating your thoughts?
Or are your thoughts creating you?'

Brooke Castillo

WHAT IS MINDSET MASTERY?

This is the chapter that most people think they don't need, but every human who has plans really does. This chapter is about Mindset Mastery, the second step of the Rent 2 Rent Success System and one of the most powerful. Mindset Mastery provides the simple, practical tools to make success inevitable for you. This will make rent to rent success easy for you and it will extend to other areas of your life.

"

The people who are
willing to work on
their development,
their minds and
their thinking first
always outperform
those who are not.

WHY IS MINDSET MASTERY IMPORTANT TO RENT 2 RENT SUCCESS?

Most of us think that it's the 'real' information – the details of the property strategy itself – rather than the 'mindset fluff' that gets the results. Yet what we've seen while guiding hundreds of people through our Rent 2 Rent Kickstarter Programme is that the people who are willing to work on their development, their minds and their thinking first always outperform those who are not. We all know people who've been on property courses and could get a PhD in rent to rent, but they haven't taken action. It's very easy to be that person. The rest of this chapter is about how *not* to be that person! This is critical to your success.

It's about how to play to win using strategies that some of the most successful people in the world use. Even if you're resistant to trying this, read through with an open mind and see whether there's anything you can take from it. I think you'll surprise yourself. And our experience is that you'll be more successful with the practical steps when you master your mind first.

HOW TO MASTER YOUR MIND

In this chapter, you'll learn how to:

1. **Stop being your own worst enemy and what you should do instead.**
2. **Think like a gamechanger.**
3. **Meet Future You.**

So, let's get into this.

Can you imagine where you'd be three months from now if you did everything you set out to do – always, and without question?

When you decide to get up early, you just do it. When you decide to exercise, you just do it. When you decide to eat healthily, you just do it. And when you decide to work on your business, you just do it.

You don't make excuses.

You don't postpone.

You don't procrastinate.

You just get on and do it.

For 99.9% of us, that doesn't happen. There are so many times we don't keep our commitments to ourselves. We prioritise our commitments to our employers, to our families, to our friends, and even to complete strangers ahead of our own. And that's why Mindset Mastery is so important.

For many of us, doing what we promise ourselves is *not* the norm as often as we'd like it to be. Being hesitant about change is part of the human condition. Doing what you promise yourself, even when it involves change, is a challenge for most of us. But when you can do this consistently, you can do something most people haven't mastered, and you will achieve results most people can't achieve.

There are tools we can use to help us keep our commitments to ourselves more often, and these are what we'll share with you in this chapter. They have helped me do more in the past 5 years than I'd done in the preceding 25! I've gone from professional procrastinator to consistent action-taker. These are the tools that helped Nicky and me get past our self-doubt and start several successful businesses, build a multi-million pound property portfolio and become mentors, coaches and authors in a short time.

Now you might be saying, 'Stephanie, I've done all this mindset stuff before.' Or, 'Nicky, I don't need this because I'm already positive. I'm already successful. I just want to make some cash.'

And you are right. You are already successful. You are already positive. And you're human, too.

Sorry to be the one to break it to you, but you need to do more. **If you're growing or changing, you need to grow your mind, too.**

It's a must. As we'll discuss below, your mind will resist you in the changes you want to make, so you need to be ready!

STOP BEING YOUR OWN WORST ENEMY

Your brain is amazing. Artificial intelligence cannot replicate the powerful complexity of your mind and the things it can do.

'If that's the case,' you ask, 'what's the problem?'

Bear with me here, because I'm about to explain something which, once you truly understand it and *live it*, can change your life, so please give me a few minutes for this.

Most of us can recognise these scenarios. You find yourself at the bottom of a packet of crisps when you promised yourself a week of healthy eating, where crisps are *not* included as one of your five a day! Or you found yourself pulling the duvet over your head when you'd planned to go to the gym early and get fit again. Or you're putting a load of washing in the machine instead of making the business calls you promised yourself.

Why do we do these things?

It's your brain's fault. That powerhouse of a brain can be used to create a life you love but, more often than not, it's left on autopilot and you've no idea what destination was loaded onto your system.

I'm simplifying this down massively, because whole books have been written on this stuff, but basically, it goes like this. Our brains have two important parts, which I'm calling your gamechanger brain and your toddler brain, which you may know as your chimp brain or primal brain.

Gamechanger brain

We have our rational brains. Your gamechanger brain is aspirational and amazing and has big goals and dreams for you. Your gamechanger brain is future focused and comes up with brilliant plans for how to make your life better a month, a year, 10 years from now. This is the brain we like to showcase proudly. Your gamechanger brain is very close to Future You. I love this brain because it inspires you to be better, to do better and to be a gamechanger in the world. Your gamechanger brain is the reason you're reading this book.

And if that were all, life would be simple. But we also have a…

Toddler brain

We evolved for survival, and most of our thinking is on automatic. Our default setting is 'NO!' – in capital letters. Our toddler brain likes things as they are. Our toddler brain wants everything *now*. Our toddler brain has little concept of tomorrow, next week or next year. And our toddler brain knows exactly what to say to get what it wants.

Explains a lot, doesn't it?

Most of us understand this at an intellectual level. And then we beat ourselves up for letting our inner toddler run the show in key areas of our lives that we want to improve.

Why have we yet again failed to stick to our plans? It's because our toddler brain has a distinct advantage: most of its 'thinking' is unconscious and immediate. So, for example, you might be leaving work but not planning to go home. As you get into your car, you remind yourself to go to the shop, yet you find yourself pulling up at home! Unconscious action. Your brain does not have to think; it 'knows' when you get in the car after work that you're going home. And you drive yourself there on autopilot.

We need to have these autopilot actions so that we don't have to consciously think to brush our teeth or make a coffee. Our brains have a lot to do each day, so we put regularly repeated actions on to autopilot to conserve energy. And your inner toddler resists considering new ideas because these can be painful, and your toddler brain's number one job is to avoid pain.

It's there to serve you and to keep you alive by:

1. **Avoiding pain**
2. **Seeking pleasure**
3. **Doing 1 and 2 using as little energy as possible.**

Your toddler brain is programmed to deal with matters of life and death. Keeping you alive is a serious business, so it pulls out all the stops to help you realise what *not* to do. Why does walking into the centre of a stage to speak to a group make you feel like you're going to die? Why does the urge to have a sweet treat sometimes feel so compelling and irresistible? So many of the negative results in our lives are caused by unconscious thinking we are unaware of. You can probably see why it's an unfair battle to expect your gamechanger brain to compete with your toddler brain in the moment and win consistently.

If we don't consciously 'programme' our chosen destination into our personal GPS, our default settings will drive us to broke, unfulfilled, couch-potatodom. It's easy to end up there if you always listen to your toddler brain, avoiding pain, seeking pleasure and using as little energy as possible.

Success is celebrated in our society because it's not the norm. When you don't consciously choose your destination, it's highly unlikely you'll end up with things that are prized, such as a successful business, financial freedom, or a fit body. These things take consistent conscious actions, which require consistent conscious thinking.

How can we change our brains to get the results we want?

We can work with our brains so that our unconscious programming is set for success rather than an autopilot destination we did not choose. Let me tell you a story to illustrate this point.

MY STORY

I understood all of the above at an intellectual level. And I'd seen great results in our businesses by consciously changing my thoughts using my gamechanger brain; gradually, over time, my toddler brain took on those thoughts and now my unconscious thoughts about business are mostly positive. It's easy to know whether your unconscious thoughts are helping you or hindering you: simply look at the results you have in your life and compare them with the results you want. I've been able to achieve a level of business and financial success that wasn't available to me before, so I can see the evidence that my unconscious thinking has improved to support me in this area.

Where this really was a battle for me, though, was with my weight. I struggled so much.

I didn't realise it at the time, but my toddler brain was totally running the show. Every time there was food nearby, my inner toddler would throw a tantrum and I'd find myself overeating. *It felt like I was eating against my will.*

I tried so hard. And I kept trying, but it was a constant uphill struggle. Even if I made a plan of what to eat, I couldn't trust myself to stick to it. I knew that if there were cakes in the office, or I received a delicious gift, or I visited a friend who'd been baking, I wouldn't stick to my plan. I was exasperated by myself. And I didn't know what to do. It felt as though I'd tried everything.

Then I heard Brooke Castillo talking about the toddler brain and I recognised myself instantly. She suggested a technique called the urge jar. It's so simple and effective. The technique involves writing down what you will eat at least 24 hours in advance. That way you can only write from your gamechanger brain and your toddler can't get involved, because it can't plan that far ahead.

Then, when the time comes to eat, you practise eating only and exactly what you said you'd eat, *no matter what else is there*.

It's like training a muscle; you're weak at first, but you grow stronger and it gets easier, and then it becomes second nature. Every action we take from our toddler brain is to avoid feeling pain, or to seek pleasure. When we have trained ourselves to feel painful or uncomfortable emotions (e.g. disappointment, boredom, shame) without taking negative actions that damage our future goals and happiness, we are on the road to Mindset Mastery.

In my forties and still struggling with what I ate, I thought I was a hopeless case, a lost cause, and that my dreams of being effortlessly slim forever were impossible for me. But using this method, I lost weight and now I feel in control of what I eat. In fact, I weigh less than when I was in my twenties! I can't tell you how good it feels to be moving into my fifties, having finally found the answer. And the answer is so incredibly simple.

What's this got to do with rent to rent?

It's the fact that your toddler brain is likely to resist you when you start anything new. We all instinctively know this. Many of us have a catalogue of failed attempts or professional-level procrastination to look back on.

When you read a book like this, you ask yourself 'will *it* work?' when what you really mean is 'will *I* work?'

When you know you want the results and you know you'll do the work, it's a no-brainer to take the steps and get the results. The successful strategy we've found in achieving this is to think like a gamechanger.

THINK LIKE A GAMECHANGER

Why is thinking so important? We often think that our feelings drive everything, and that our feelings are 'the truth'. What we sometimes forget is that we can change our feelings with our thoughts.

Here's how it works:

, Your thoughts drive your feelings.

, Your feelings drive your actions.

, Your actions drive your results.

In short, your thoughts create your results.

For any aspect of your life where your results are not where you want them to be, it's because your thinking isn't where it needs to be to achieve different results.

You have the potential to achieve things that feel unachievable by practising thinking consciously. That's what we call 'gamechanger thinking'. This process will help you to do what you set out to do and move you on to great results. Thinking like a gamechanger helps you to put in the reps to build up so that your toddler brain helps you achieve success, rather than hindering you.

I'm going to introduce three useful and empowering thoughts for gamechanger thinking, and they will help you to improve your results. Remember, though, that you can choose thoughts that work for you – if these aren't quite right for you, choose thoughts that work better for you.

Let's move on to the first gamechanger thought.

Thought 1: I am always there for me, no matter what

This one invites you to be your own best friend. You will be your ally, your supporter, your cheerleader. You will be your expert, your thinker. You will be the expert on what's best for you. So often, we aren't there for ourselves. We check out. We say, 'I can't.' We say, 'I don't know.' We hide from our problems. We don't have faith in our ability to think, to work things out, to get better. To succeed in living a bigger life.

Become a rock for you. Know you will always be there for you. Know you can always rely on you. *No matter what.*

The main reason people don't succeed is that they give up. Don't give up. The *no matter what* is there because the times when you most need to be there for you are the times when it will be the hardest: the times when you blame yourself for past decisions, when you criticise your inability to stick to the plan, when you've made a misstep. Those are the times you need to be there for you in a bigger and bolder way. To encourage yourself to keep going, to take the very next step and then the one after that. It's times like these that separate the winners from the stoppers.

If beliefs come in such as:

, I can't do this.
, I'm not good enough.
, I should just stick to my job, who am I trying to kid?

lovingly remind yourself of your new thought. Some people like to think about it as looking after their toddler. Look after your inner toddler. Know that we all experience this. When you feel scared or stuck, be compassionate, be loving and reassure your toddler that you will always be there for them, no matter what. Then get your gamechanger brain in gear. Make a plan. And stick to it.

You will always be there for you, no matter what.

Thought 2: I am resourceful

Many times, we let a lack of resources stop us. But lack of resources is a myth. I must admit, I didn't agree with this idea at first; it seems obvious that some people lack resources and others don't, and I often felt I didn't have enough. Many of us feel we'd be more successful if only we had the right resources.

However, knowing what I know now, I can see it's not a lack of resources that holds us back – it's lack of resourcefulness. We need to grow our ability to harness the resources of others to create win-wins. We can become more resourceful and learn the skills to attract more resources to ourselves.

Even though we may resist this idea at first, we know in our hearts it's true. As you look around your network of family and friends, you will see examples of people who started off with very little and, through resourcefulness, now have a lot.

 Most of us don't lack resources. We lack resourcefulness.

Let's look now at the obstacles that are standing in your way. Often these things exist more in our minds than in reality. But we still have to deal with them. We all have them.

What are the things that you feel really hold you back? Here are some answers that people have given in our coaching sessions.

, I haven't got time to run a business. I'm looking after my family and I've got three kids and a husband.

, I'm too old to get started.

, I'm too young to get started.

, I don't have the skills.

, I don't have the property experience.

, I don't have the intelligence.

, I speak with an accent.

I can understand why people think these are logical and valid reasons.

These things can stop you – if you decide to let them. The thing to remember is that there are people successfully running rent to rent businesses despite all of these 'obstacles'. Whether you decide to see something as an obstacle is actually a choice you make. It's not the truth. Or at least, it's not the truth for everyone. Others are succeeding with the very things you are calling obstacles.

 There's a way for you to succeed from the exact circumstances you have at the moment. Other people are doing it right now, and you can too.

'When we are no longer able to change a situation, we are challenged to change ourselves.'

— Viktor E Frankl

Start where you are with what you have, and do the best you can. Do look at your resources and obstacles. Whatever they are, there is a way to succeed. If you decide to.

You are resourceful.

Thought 3: I am unstoppable

The third gamechanger thought is about the quiet power of persistence. Most of us give up too easily. Thinking 'I am unstoppable' is a way of tapping into your persistence to keep going until you succeed. The successful players are the ones who stay in the game and remain on the field of play long enough to go from rookie to rockstar.

We see what we focus on, so tune in to what you want and commit yourself to keeping going until you get there. Become unstoppable.

If I say, 'Don't think about baby hippos bathing in pink champagne,' what happens? Your brain will solve problems that you give it, and it's very efficient. Have you noticed that if you give your brain a question before you go to sleep often enough, one morning you wake up with the perfect answer? If you ask your brain to find reasons why you can't do something, it will help you. And if you ask your brain to find ways for you to succeed, it will help you.

Focus on where you want to go with your rent to rent business. Focus on your deeper desires as well. One critical thing that will help you along the way is to ask better questions.

Instead of saying:

, I can't do this.
, I don't have enough time.
, I can't afford this.

Say:

, I'm so proud I tried to do this. It didn't go as well as I'd hoped, though; how could I do it better next time?
, How could I make more time to do the things that will give me the life I want?
, How could I afford this?

Asking these types of questions opens your mind to possibility. Can you see the difference? These questions help you unlock the power in your mind.

Remind yourself daily that you are unstoppable. Set yourself up for success. Keep taking the steps, keep working the system, and you will get there. All you need to do – and this can sometimes be the difficult bit – is believe in your own success, believe in yourself, get out of your own way and follow the plan, even though it might feel uncomfortable at the start.

'It ain't over til you win!'

— Les Brown

You are unstoppable.

Mark Fitzgerald

For Mark Fitzgerald, his first property didn't come immediately.

'It took four months to get my first deal, so it didn't happen straight away. I was seeing properties, but they weren't quite right for me for various reasons. I was beginning to lose hope when I got my first deal and then went on to secure eight properties in eight months! Working on my mindset really helped me to take action every day, even the days I didn't really want to, and become more resilient.'

Do it your way!

Choose the thoughts that are right for *you*. If, for example, the thought of being unstoppable feels too bold at the moment, try alternatives until you have one that is right for you. You must find it encouraging and believable. For example, you may prefer:

, I will keep going.
, I will work it out.
, I am capable.

Choose what works for you, and harness the incredible power of your mind to take you wherever you'd like to go.

MEET FUTURE YOU!

The idea of training your thinking can feel a little overwhelming for most of us. It can feel unachievable, especially when you're new to this, so I'm giving you a useful practical way to get started without needing years of therapy! I know this one might sound a little strange at first, so stay with me here; it really will make a difference for you, I promise. In fact, this one could massively alter the direction of your life.

We all have a Future Us.

Your Future You exists only in your mind, of course. You believe that tomorrow you will wake up and do the things you have planned. You have thoughts about who Future You will be tomorrow. Mostly, though, our thoughts about what we'll do tomorrow, or next year, or in 10 years' time, are constrained by the evidence of what we did yesterday, a year ago, 5 years ago. That's why most people end up doing the same thing year in and year out. When you talk to most successful people, you'll find they are consciously thinking about their future. They are creating it in their minds first. Like athletes visualising winning a race, they are visualising winning at life in whatever way is important to them.

Most of the things you can do for Future You today – such as eating well, exercising, or saving and investing – might be boring or uncomfortable, which makes it easy *not* to do them. When you get to know Future You intimately, you're more likely to do uncomfortable or painful things for them – I mean, you. You make the call, you send the letter, you deliver your social pitch, because you know in one month, one year or five years from now, Future You will look back on this moment and be glad you did.

EXERCISE

Future You

Doing this simple exercise will help you imagine how your Future You will look back in a year, or in 5 or 10 years, and thank you for taking action now to make your financial future better.

You can download our **Future You Worksheet** at: **rent2rent-success.com/essentials**

▶ *Action*

Think ahead to your Future You and list your deepest desires.

This is where we are going to delve down into your deep desires. The road to success has lots of bumps in it because… well, that's life. And to keep things going, it's good to plug into what we really, really want. So, think about why you are doing this. You might say, 'to have more money', but think about why you want more money.

- How would you change your life if money and time were no object?
- Who would you become?
- What would you have, if you could have anything that you wanted in life?

Think about what excites you, what makes you really happy.

- Is it freedom from the nine to five job you dislike?
- Is it having more time with your family and your children?
- Is it the opportunity to travel the world?

Really open your mind to think about what you *really* want and write down the things that come into your mind.

- Who do you want to be in five years' time?
- What do you want for Future You?

Get it all out and written down; the worksheet will help you.

▶ *Action*

Now, let's add some costs to your Future You life.

Think about how much that life will cost and how much money you will need. Work out the monthly cost for each item on your desired life list.

Sometimes it can be surprising how little money you would actually need each month to be able to live your dream life. Many people find that they could live the life of their dreams for between £5k and £10k a month. And even if yours is more, it's achievable once you start off in property.

Our first five properties gave us a cashflow of £3,633 per month. Mark's first five properties give him a cashflow of £3,250 per month. You don't need many to give you a great additional income.

Now, when you're thinking like a gamechanger, always keep Future You in mind and think how grateful you'll be for everything you're doing now.

Reflect on your Future You. Think about the incredible things you'll be doing that you can't quite believe right now, and thank yourself for taking action to get yourself there – because, no matter what, you won't let yourself down. You are resourceful and you are unstoppable.

SUMMARY OF MINDSET MASTERY

Well done for sticking with this chapter. Working on your mindset doesn't always feel easy, yet it is critical to your success and makes the rest of the process much easier.

In this chapter, we discussed:

, How you can take a step by step approach to understanding the impact of Mindset Mastery.

, How you can stop being your own worst enemy.

, How you can think like a gamechanger by consciously focusing on thoughts that move you closer to your goals.

We discussed three useful thoughts:

, I am always there for me, no matter what.

, I am resourceful.

, I am unstoppable.

We also introduced some powerful exercises to bring conscious clarity to the Future You that you want to create for yourself.

TOP TIP

Remember to offer yourself grace.

You don't go for the heavy weights when it's your first time in the gym. You pick up the beginner weights and then, as you become stronger, you move on to the heavier ones.

So, for example, if you've previously had trouble taking action on something and now believe you're a procrastinator, it's important to take the next step from where you are. For example, you could set yourself a goal: I will focus for 30 minutes, three days per week, and build up to an hour each working day. You could progress from there rather than going straight to 'I will focus all day, every day', failing, and giving up.

Start where you are, with what you have, and do what you can. Don't expect to climb a mountain in one leap. The way to climb a mountain is to take the step that's right in front of you. And repeat it.

You will always be there for you, no matter what.

You are resourceful.

You are unstoppable.

Now that your mind is prepared, you're ready to fly. Let's prepare for take-off in the next chapter, which is all about setting up your business.

Note to Self: You are going to make yourself so proud.

STEP 3
MIND YOUR BUSINESS

Start your business quickly, legally and inexpensively, even if you have no business or property experience.

'Those who are successful overcome their fears and take action. Those who aren't submit to their fears and live with regrets.'

Jay-Z

WHAT IS MIND YOUR BUSINESS?

Mind Your Business is pure gold. It's a set of essential actions to start your business quickly, legally and inexpensively, even if you have no business or property experience. Confusion over what needs to be done and fear of falling foul of the law can stop people from starting. Or people spend hundreds of pounds on things they *don't* need and entirely miss what they *do* need!

WHY IS MIND YOUR BUSINESS IMPORTANT TO RENT 2 RENT SUCCESS?

It's fundamental to get your business set up right, the first time. You'll be able to set up your rent to rent business within days and weeks, instead of many months, years or never. And you'll know that you're following a proven system for success.

Now, we're going to walk you through the business setup steps to rent to rent success – the 4 Cs:

1. **Company setup basics – get set up**
2. **Contact details – get contactable**
3. **Clear message – get clarity**
4. **Compliance – get legal.**

I don't want you to underestimate the importance of this information. Once you know it, it becomes 'obvious'. This is your no confusion setup for success.

Let's get down to business.

1ST C: COMPANY SETUP BASICS – GET SET UP

It's important to get this right so that everything is set up cor-rectly from the start. That will mean you'll have everything you need in place to be compliant and that you won't waste money on anything you don't need.

Limited company or sole trader?

The first step is to decide whether you want to be a limited company or a sole trader. Either is fine, and the choice is yours. It partly depends on your current financial position. If you're a higher rate taxpayer or already have a business, it's defi-nitely worth speaking to your accountant. A limited company is often better for higher rate taxpayers, because corporation tax is significantly less than their personal tax.

Limited companies have limited liability, which means that if your company owed money, it couldn't be taken from you personally, only from your company. However, there are legal requirements for a limited company to publish accounts and other information, so having a limited company will cost more in terms of having professionals to assist you to do this.

As a general rule, if you'd like to build a business and replace your income, then a limited company is more appropriate. If you just want to have one or two properties for a little extra income, then perhaps setting up as a sole trader would work for you. If you're unsure, you can start as a sole trader and set up a limited company later.

People do look to us to advise which is 'best', but the truth is that neither is 'best' for everyone. It depends on your circumstances, goals and preferences.

The important thing is to make a decision and move forward. You can change in the future if you need to.

Business values and business name

As part of choosing your business name, you should also choose your business values. You might be wondering why business values are important. Why can't you just choose a business name and move on? Well, your business values give you direction and clarity. When you are totally clear about what your business stands for, speaking to others is so much easier. And it creates an ethical compass that will show you when you're going in the right direction. Our values for HMO Heaven are *excellence*, *improvement* and *care*. They are values we felt were lacking in lettings, and they fit in with what we wanted to offer, which was a heavenly experience for everyone we worked with, built on caring about people.

When you know your values, you're not starting from scratch each time; the fundamentals of your business promise are already in place. Choosing your business values helps you develop a clear message, making it easy to share with others what you do. It's something that makes you stand out, because most people don't do this, and it helps attract the right people to you: people who believe the same things you do.

EXERCISE
Your Business Values

Your business values provide direction and clarity for your business. They are the glue that underpins everything you do, and they are the standard by which your business will operate.

Download our **Your Business Values Worksheet** from **rent-2rentsuccess.com/essentials** and let's define what your business stands for.

Choose your business values

▶ *Action*

Brainstorm and write down words that resonate with you when pondering the following questions:

1. **What are the values of businesses you admire?**
2. **What attributes do you dislike in a business?**
3. **What are the values of your perfect employee?**
4. **What attributes make a challenging employee?**
5. **Consider the values (attributes) you have written down, and circle the words that reflect the standards and culture you would want for your business.**

Add any additional values doing the exercise has triggered for you and circle them.

Identify your top three business values

▶ *Action*

Identify your top three business values from your circled values. Remember there is no wrong answer. Your values are personal, they are yours. If they suit you, and the standard by which you want to operate and manage your business, they are 100% perfect.

Test your chosen business values

▶ *Action*

Look at your values and ask yourself the following questions:

1. **Would my business values attract my perfect customer?**
2. **Would my business values inspire my team to deliver in a way that would delight my customer?**
3. **Do my business values make me feel good?**

▶ *Action*

Take a break, have a stretch, make a coffee, and then have another look at your chosen values. If you are still happy, well done – you've got your business values!

Remember that, like so many of the moving parts of your business, you should revisit this exercise periodically to retest your business values and ensure that, as you and your business grow, they remain valid and relevant.

Set up your limited company, if applicable

Now's the time to set up a limited company, if you have chosen to. You can do this quickly and easily online.

SIC code (standard industrial classification code)

You'll need to choose a SIC code to set up your limited company. SIC codes are used to classify the business activities of a company. Companies House and other government bodies use them to identify what a company does.

The SIC code for rent to rent is 68209 for 'other letting and operating of own or leased real estate'.

Open a bank account for your business

If you're starting a limited company, you must open a business bank account in the same name. If you're starting a sole trader business, you can set up a bank account for your business or you can use your existing personal bank account. I strongly suggest the former; having a separate bank account makes every aspect of business oversight and administration easier.

STUART BOWKER'S STORY

I came to rent to rent as someone who has some buy-to-let properties with my wife and a real interest in property for the future of my family, having worked with commercial and retail property in various roles for a few years.

It's a big step to start your own business, and I have had a couple of attempts at making it happen. Working through the programme and system with R2R Kickstarter, I was able to implement these systems. Stephanie and Nicky keep it simple, and the mindset element is really accessible and effective. I have been able to keep my focus and eye on the small picture that will drive the long-term results. It has been great to build my network within the Kickstarter Community; it only takes one like-minded connection to make a huge difference to your outlook and confidence.

2ⁿᵈ C: CONTACT DETAILS – GET CONTACTABLE

This step is all about setting up the contact details for your business. This is important, so you can ensure you have them all ready to go before you start marketing.

Telephone number

You can organise this in whatever way works for you. However, I can offer a few examples of what has worked for other people we've taught. You can keep things simple and use your existing mobile to start off with, or you might prefer a new mobile. It's relatively inexpensive to buy a new phone for business purposes, if you want to keep things separate. There is also a school of thought that says a business with a landline looks more 'established', which is helpful for your website and business cards. You can buy a virtual landline inexpensively.

Website domain

Buy a domain for your website.

Email address

You will also want a company email address. Let's use the example of Femi at Lovely Homes. Instead of **femi@gmail.com**, he would have **femi@lovelyhomes.com**, which looks more professional. I think this is worth doing as it's inexpensive and straightforward to do and will help your business look professional.

Social media

I hesitated about including social media, because the temptation is to invest a lot of time on it. The return on the time invested in creating a Facebook page or Instagram account for your new business is very small at the start, as very few people will see your posts. However, on balance, it is good in the longer term. For more short-term impact, I encourage you to show your property progress on your personal social media profiles too. Use your personal profile to tell the story of your whole life, not just the non-work parts. That way, you can share what you're doing with your network. It's an important part of becoming known for what you do, which we'll discuss more in Magnetic Marketing.

3ᴿᴰ C: CLEAR MESSAGE – GET CLARITY

This step is about creating clarity in what you do so that it's easier to share it with the world – or at least the landlords and agents you talk to, and everyone else in your network.

Here, you'll craft your offer, create your logo, print your business cards and publish your webpage.

This part is important first and foremost in what it does for *you*. It gives you clarity, which gives you confidence, which helps you to attract your perfect landlords and letting agents more easily. You may feel tempted to skip the first part of this step, so I want to reassure you that being clear about what your business offers will have a huge impact on your effectiveness in communicating your offer, and ultimately in your success.

What your business offers

The objective here is for you to write a few paragraphs about what you offer landlords, and a separate piece on what you offer agents. This is to enable you to follow up quickly by email whenever needed. You don't want to have to sit down to craft an email from scratch each time! I know from bitter experience that delay in following up can cause you to miss opportunities. You need something that can be copied and pasted quickly.

You might be good with words and love writing, in which case this will be your thing. But even if you think you're not a great writer, just get something down on paper. It will evolve over time. It doesn't need to be perfect, but it does need to be done; progress, not perfection. You don't have to have it designed. For now, all you need is the words written in a document, a few paragraphs that clearly explain what you do and what you offer.

Looking good – do you really need to?

The next three parts of this step – your logo, your business card and your webpage – are all about looking good, so are they essential? No – but they are definitely recommended. You can write to landlords, visit agents, and get a deal without them, but we believe that the cumulative effect of having them in place helps you look more professional and, as a bonus, helps you feel more confident.

In the digital age, many people say a business card, in particular, is not essential, and I agree with them. However, it's useful for us because it's something physical we can leave with landlords and agents or give to new contacts at networking events. Ultimately, it's your business and your choice. For a little extra time and a little money, we believe it's well worth the investment.

Logo

You can use online designers or, if you prefer to DIY, you can use one of the many free tools. We have a list of tools we recommend on the **Rockstar Essentials** website[18].

Business card

Once you're happy with your logo, move on to your business card. Because we know that things will change, do a small print run to start with. The number of cards you order depends on how active you expect to be in the next few months.

Webpage

The last step is creating a webpage. A web presence is important so that Google knows what your business is and who you are. What you're going to create is a simple webpage so that landlords, agents or people who meet you at networking events can visit your webpage and find you there! The reason I'm calling this a web*page* rather than a web*site* is because I want you to get this done quickly. I want you to get it up and running so that you can move forward with completing your first deal. What I don't want is you spending aeons making your webpage 'perfect' and all the while *not* doing the things that will help you to get your first deal. The main thing to remember is to *get it done*! It doesn't need to be a masterpiece; it just needs to do the job. The job is showing that you exist and are credible. Create a very simple webpage.

Here, we walked through getting your business out of your mind and into the world. It's an exciting step seeing your ideas become a reality. It's one of the joys of entrepreneurship.

Now, let's move on to the final part.

4ᵀᴴ C: COMPLIANCE – GET LEGAL

This is the part that people worry about the most, because no one wants to be found to have an illegal business. Don't let those who seek to scare you from getting started put you off. We'll take you through our simple process, step by step. Once you've completed these steps, you're fully compliant and ready to roll.

Here's what you'll need to consider:

- Insurance
- Information Commissioner's Office
- Property Redress Scheme
- Client Money Protection
- Local landlord/licensing schemes in your area
- National Residential Landlords Association

Let's take them one by one.

Insurance: public liability insurance and professional indemnity insurance

You will need to find a specialist insurance broker who understands rent to rent.

Professional indemnity insurance

Professional indemnity insurance protects you against claims made against you for financial loss; for example, if a landlord says a repair that you were contractually required to do wasn't done or was completed to a poor standard, leaving them needing to fix it themselves.

Public liability insurance

Public liability insurance protects you against claims made against you for damage or physical injury; for example, if a prospective tenant slipped in one of your properties and they claimed against you.

Employers' liability insurance

Similar to public liability, but it is only required if you have employees; for example, it will be required if an employee injures themselves whilst at work. You and your fellow directors are not classified as employees.

It is a legal requirement to have professional indemnity and public liability insurance, and employers' liability insurance if you have employees.

Information Commissioner's Office

Under the Data Protection (Charges and Information) Regulations 2018, individuals and organisations that process personal data need to pay a data protection fee to the Information Commissioner's Office (ICO), unless they are exempt. Rent to rent is not considered exempt.

It is a legal requirement to be a member of the Information Commissioner's Office. If you do not register, you may be fined by the ICO.

Property Redress Scheme

A redress scheme is a scheme that allows consumers to escalate a complaint they have against a member of the scheme. The main purpose of the redress scheme is to resolve or settle unresolved complaints from consumers who have suffered a loss as a result of the actions of the member.

The Property Redress Scheme (PRS) or the Property Ombudsman are your choices.

It is a legal requirement to be a member of a property redress scheme.

Client Money Protection

Client Money Protection (CMP) is a scheme that reimburses landlords and tenants should an agent misappropriate their rent, deposit or other client funds, or go into administration. From 1 April 2019, it has been a legal requirement for property agents to have Client Money Protection.

If we were a traditional letting agent managing a landlord's property and charging the landlord a fee, rather than paying guaranteed rent, we would need CMP for the rent we collect. However, as we do not charge a landlord fee, this is not applicable to our rent to rent business. The PRS confirms this in its guide *An Agent Guide to Rent to Rent or Guaranteed Rent*.[19]

Local requirements

It's worth checking the regulations in the area where you are operating, as some councils already make CMP mandatory as a term of giving an HMO licence.

Future changes

We are watching this area closely for any changes, and we'll update the **Rockstar Essentials website** to keep you informed. It's also worth subscribing to *The Rent 2 Rent Success Podcast* and the *Rent 2 Rent Success* YouTube channel, so you can keep up to date with all things rent to rent.

Local landlord/licensing schemes in your area

There may also be local landlord or licensing schemes in your rent to rent area(s) that you are required to join, so check with your local council and ensure that you have registered for any required schemes. This will also be very helpful in your marketing and in demonstrating you are a professional company.

Landlords' Association

Optionally, you can join a landlords' association to get expertise, support and resources. The British Landlord Association is a free option, or for a fee you can become a member of the National Residential Landlords' Association.

SHARI MCLAREN-STERLING'S STORY

When I joined R2R Kickstarter, I'd already set up a company on Companies House, but I hadn't done things in terms of getting a business bank account yet. I had quite a lot missing from the business setup, so that's why I was appreciative of the guidance. It didn't take long to set everything up – two weeks, at most, and that was only because it took a while to set up the business bank account.

Shari is based in the Midlands. She and her business partner, Jules, quickly went on to secure two properties and over £800 per month in cashflow. You can meet them and hear more of their story on the **Rockstar Essentials website**[20].

SUMMARY OF MIND YOUR BUSINESS

In this chapter, we discussed:

- The 4 Cs of how to set up your business, from company setup basics right through to compliance.
- The biggest takeaway here: the need to move forward quickly and to *get it done*.

Great! That's everything you need to set up your business. I'm really looking forward to moving on now with you to Magnetic Marketing and taking things to the next level, where we are going to start getting out there and talking to landlords and letting agents.

STEP 4
MAGNETIC MARKETING

Attract owners and agents to you with our unique Magnetic Marketing methods, which work even if you hate selling or are shy.

'I've learned that people will forget what you said, people will forget what you did, but people will never forget how you made them feel.'

— Maya Angelou

WHAT IS MAGNETIC MARKETING?

It's your secret sauce, and it'll be irresistible to your perfect customers. We're going to discuss how to attract your perfect landlords and letting agents in a way that clearly speaks to what your customers really want.

You might be excited about this – or you might have concerns about 'selling'. It's true that many people see selling as sleazy or uncomfortable. We're going to show you simple strategies for success, even if you are shy or hate the idea of selling.

WHY IS MAGNETIC MARKETING IMPORTANT TO RENT 2 RENT SUCCESS?

It's hugely important because if you have an incredible service that no one knows about, your business won't flourish. We all know of companies with a mediocre service but magnificent marketing who do incredibly well. Attracting the right customers is an important part of your success. The process we're going to show you means you never have to sell in a way that is sleazy – and you don't have to be anyone but *you!*

This chapter goes beyond rent to rent; the methods we teach here are marketing fundamentals that will help you become more compelling, whatever you're doing. We'll talk about becoming irresistible to your perfect customers.

"

People buy with
emotions and they
justify with logic.

"

HOW TO MAGNETISE YOUR MARKETING

In this chapter, you will learn:

1. **Our definition of Magnetic Marketing**
2. **Magnetic Marketing for landlords**
3. **Magnetic Marketing for letting agents**
4. **How to build likeability and trust quickly**
5. **The power of your social pitch.**

Let's get started!

OUR DEFINITION OF MAGNETIC MARKETING

When you become magnetic, the results are incredible. Our theory is based on one hugely important and undeniable truth – a truth many people fail to take into account in their marketing, and so they get terrible results.

So what is this undeniable truth?

People buy with emotions and they justify with logic.

Landlords and agents are human, too; they start with their feelings. We all do, even though many of us don't recognise this in ourselves. To be successful, you need to tap into what your customers are *really* looking for. What emotions are driving them? And remember: sometimes, they won't be consciously aware of this.

Why did our first landlord choose us, when other people offered him over £200 a month more in rent? It's not just about logic; it's also about emotion. Security, trust, relationships are all real drivers. Most landlords who come to you will already have tried a letting agent and had something go wrong. The things that went wrong cost them time and money and peace of mind.

When you tap into what your customers are really looking for (and also the things they want to avoid), your customers become magnetically attracted to you. What I'm going to show you here is how to create something so attractive that it's as irresistible as a cute dachshund puppy.

It's your secret sauce. It'll create attraction. You'll know it's working when people start approaching you about what you do. We're going to discuss how to define what you do in a way that is different to what other people are doing, and that speaks to what your customers really, really want.

Here's our definition:

Magnetic Marketing attracts your perfect customers to you by clearly stating your customers' problems and your solution using your customers language.

Let's start off with Magnetic Marketing for landlords.

MAGNETIC MARKETING FOR LANDLORDS

Before we go into how best to market to landlords, here's a quick reminder of what landlords want:

, They want their rent paid on time.
, They want their property looked after.

And most importantly, and often overlooked:

, They want minimal risk in any transaction.

Let's move on to the best way to attract landlords to you with landlord letters.

How to write irresistible landlord letters

Now, this may seem counterintuitive. Why on earth would we be sending letters in a digital age? Quite simply because we have the names and addresses of HMO landlords, and we don't have their email addresses. For this reason, landlord letters are *the* best strategy for getting direct to landlord deals. The name and address details are publicly available and can be requested from the relevant council. And a perfectly crafted Magnetic Marketing letter is a way for you to speak directly to your ideal customers.

Most of our new properties come from this method. Landlord letters – personalised, printed and posted via an automated process (detailed on the **Rockstar Essentials website**[21]) – cost us less than the price of a first-class stamp for each letter. So far, we've spent a total of £2,631.72 on letters, and brought in contracts worth over £2m. That's a whopping 75,895% return on investment! I think you'll agree, it's phenomenally successful.

The question I then get is, 'But do letters really work? So many people are sending letters now – how do I stand out from the crowd?'

The secret to letters that work

The secret lies in clearly solving landlord problems, using their language. It's about creating enough interest in your solution to cause them to phone you to find out more.

'That's so obvious, Stephanie!' I hear you cry. 'That's not a secret!'

Well, if that's the case, why do I see so many letters that miss the mark? Before I move on, I need to show you what not to do.

What not to do

One of our landlords keeps all the letters he receives from people wanting to rent his HMO, and recently he brought a batch in. I was totally shocked that about 80% of them had very similar wording. Here's what not to do if you want to get the best possible results:

What not to do – example letter 1

Here's an excerpt:

We are looking to acquire eight domestic HMO/multi-let properties in the area, and we are aware that some landlords are looking to get out of the business, and we were wonder-

ing if you were considering, or would consider selling any of your properties...

You can see the full letter on the **Rockstar Essentials website**[22].

What's wrong with this letter? First of all, it's focused too much on the 'we'. It's focused too much on the investors who are writing this letter and what their needs are and what they're looking to do. 'We are looking... we are aware... we were wondering.' To have maximum impact, your letter needs to *focus on what your reader, the landlord, wants*, and how you can help them to achieve it with your solution.

The next thing is that using phrases like 'HMO/multi-lets' is clunky. *Make your language conversational*, as if you are talking to landlords individually, rather than using 'business speak'.

What not to do – example letter 2

The second example starts off on a very bad foot. It says:

I hope you don't mind me writing to you. I found your contact details on the Greenland council online register of HMO landlords as well.

You can see the full letter on the **Rockstar Essentials website.**

What's wrong with it? The opening line is apologetic and unnecessary, and it positions the writer as being of low value. You have a great solution for a difficult problem, so *don't apologise for sharing it with people.*

Don't send one of those letters that focus more on the writer's needs than the reader's. We all feel drawn to someone who understands us, someone who can serve us and someone we trust. Be that person.

 It's challenging for HMO landlords to find a trusted person or company to manage their HMOs to a consistently high standard. You are that person, and that's why your offer is compelling.

So... what do I write?

People then say, 'Well, OK. I'll try it. What do I write? Where do I start?'

Sitting in front of a blank piece of paper can feel daunting. Even professional writers can find it difficult. In your first sentence, you need to show that you understand the challenges the landlord is facing. Your mantra for this whole letter is: 'It's all about them. It's not about me.'

 The only job of your first sentence is to get your reader to want to read the next sentence.

First of all, you want to talk about the pain point or solution statement. Don't open by talking about you, and what your goals are. For example, in 'What not to do' – Example 1, the writer's goal was to 'acquire eight domestic HMO/multi-let properties in the area'. Talk about problems that your reader, the landlord, is concerned about.

The next step is to show how your specialised solution delivers total relief. You need to explain how your solution resolves the pain point.

 Show the sizzle and not the steak. Don't overwhelm people with detail at this stage.

Keep it simple. Explain just enough that your reader wants to call you to find out more. Talk about your readers' problems/goals and how you can help them to achieve those goals. Simply, we all want what we want **with simplicity**. We want someone who understands us, someone who can serve us with a solution that we can *easily* see will help us with the problem we have.

 Let your reader know the next step.

You need to give your reader a clear call to action. We've found the best one to be a phone call. A good call to action excites people's curiosity and makes them feel compelled to pick up the phone and find out more.

HOW DO I PUT ALL THAT TOGETHER?

Now, I'm going to give you an example of one of our letters where we put these things into practice, so you can see the sort of things you might include.

Magnetic Marketing landlord letter

Download the full letter on the **Rockstar Essentials website**

This is the first letter we sent out.

We got our first two properties from a letting agent and, once we'd seen that rent to rent really worked, we decided to send out a landlord letter. This letter brought in three of our highest cashflow properties, including an eight-bed HMO and nine self-contained flats.

You can see that we clearly talk about some problems landlords may have, and our solution. At the end, there is a call to action: 'call us for a chat and find out how we can make your life easier'. Since writing this letter, we've made our call to action more direct; for example, 'call us now to find out how much guaranteed rent we can give you for your HMO'. This is stronger as it provokes curiosity.

The Main Thing

The main thing is to send your letters. Landlords can't ring you if they don't know you exist, so let them know. Send your letters and let them know very soon. We've included some information and resources about letters – including one of our own contract-winning letters – on our **Rockstar Essentials website** at **rent2rentsuccess.com/essentials.**

Other ways to contact landlords

In this book, we're focusing on the things to do that will really move the needle. Landlord letters are the most effective way we've found to contact landlords directly (i.e. not through a letting agent). However, there are others you can try too. These methods leverage online and in-person opportunities:

- Contacting landlords on online property portals, such as SpareRoom, OpenRent, Gumtree, Zoopla and Rightmove.

- Attending local landlord events – these are distinct from property investor networking events. Both are good, but the local landlord events tend to include more people who may be open to working with you.

- Placing Facebook ads – some people have had success with this, though I do warn you that if you're not an ads expert, it's best to seek specialist help; it's easy to throw money away. I encourage you to try organic (i.e. free!) methods first. Find out what works and then, once you're gaining leads and customers that way, you'll have a better chance to speed things up effectively with paid advertising.

- Using property ~~sourcerers~~ sourcers – be careful before you buy a deal, and ensure that you use our Deal Analyser (see Step 5) to ensure that it is a good deal before parting with any money. Or better still, use the information in this book and source your own properties.

Now let's move on to letting agents.

MAGNETIC MARKETING FOR LETTING AGENTS

We talked about letting agents, and the myth that no letting agent would want to work with you, in Mythbusters. In fact, letting agents can be a big part of your business. They have a flow of properties, so a good relationship with one agent can bring you a stream of properties. But most people don't understand how to work with letting agents, and they kill their chances of success without realising it.

What letting agents want

Letting agents want the same things as landlords: the rent paid on time, the property looked after, and minimal risk. There's one crucial addition, though: agents want their fees paid, too. Agents tend to be more risk-averse than landlords as they don't want to have to explain to a landlord that they made a bad choice of 'tenant'.

If you feel terrified about the thought of talking to agents, rest assured that most people do. But in the end, they've found it's much easier than they thought.

BRENDA OKANDJU'S STORY

I was nervous about it [talking to agents] at first, but what I've found is that, when it comes to the agents, relationship building is important. When agents know they can trust you, then they'll give you more opportunities. Now we find agents are calling us letting us know what's available and asking whether particular properties would work for us.

Brenda's first property was in Kensington in London; rent to rent works really well in London. Her very first deal brought cashflow of over £1,000 per month. You can watch Brenda's story on the **Rockstar Essentials website**[23].

How letting agents' fees work

Before I move on to talk about marketing to agents, I want to explain about how their fees work, as I know people are often confused about how exactly letting agents work and how you fit into the process.

There are two main ways in which agents work:

Fully managed with a monthly service fee. For example, a recurring monthly fee of 10% + VAT of rents received.

Here is a typical arrangement if you work with a letting agent fully managing a property:

- You are the 'tenant'.
- You pay the agent the rent as normal.
- The agent keeps the fee they agreed with the landlord (e.g. 10% + VAT).
- The agent pays the remaining rent to the landlord.
- The agent will organise repairs and the landlord will pay for them.

Tenant find only with a one-off fixed fee; for example, a one-off payment of 50% of the first month's rent + VAT

Here is another typical arrangement if you work with a letting agent on a tenant find only basis:

- You are the 'tenant'.
- The landlord pays the agent an agreed one-off fee for finding a tenant and doing the paperwork (e.g. 50% of the first month's rent + VAT).
- The agent introduces you to the landlord and you deal with the landlord directly from then on.
- You pay rent to the landlord. The agent receives a one-off fee from the landlord and then doesn't receive any fees ongoing.
- You will organise repairs and pay for the minor ones, and the landlord will pay for more significant repairs.

These are *typical* arrangements. Of course, things can be done differently if it is agreed by all parties.

Letting agents much prefer to 'fully manage' a property, because it gives them monthly recurring revenue that could go on for years. The value of their business is tied to the number of fully managed properties they have under contract. With a typical high street agent having staff costs and office overheads, their ability to generate cashflow for their business and sleep easily at night depends on the number of recurring-revenue fully managed properties they have. This need is even more acute with the introduction of the Tenant Fees Ban in 2019 (as part of the Tenant Fees Act 2019), which banned most tenant fees.[24]

You can see why a letting agent would not want to lose any of their fully managed properties!

The magic words every agent wants to hear

Looking at how agents work and what they want, you'll realise two things:

1. It's important to understand whether the property is fully managed or tenant find only without spooking the agent!

2. You need to stand out from others by delivering exactly what agents want clearly and quickly. If they have any doubts about whether they'll get their commission with you, they won't work with you.

Fully managed

'…your fees will be paid as normal.'

Tenant find only

'…we pay a thank you fee of £xxx for every property we take on via your agency.'

Or, if you *really* want to sweeten the deal, you can offer the agent a monthly commission for as long as you have the contract. This is what most people will not be doing. And if you can serve the agent in this way, they're more likely to go the extra mile in seeking out properties for you, and you can still deal directly with the landlord.

Agents want to let properties quickly without any costs or hassle, and you can help them do that.

 Imagine you can call someone and work with them where they do the work and you get paid! That's what agents have with you.

Independent letting agents may be more willing to try alternatives such as rent to rent. However, don't rule out chains; they are often franchises, run by business people rather than employees, and might be willing to try something new. Our first two properties were from a big national franchise agent who was working on a tenant find only basis.

HOW TO BUILD LIKEABILITY AND TRUST QUICKLY

Experience is not the most important thing – if it were, no one would ever get their first deal – but we need to be able to convince landlords and agents that we are a minimal-risk option. The two most important things are likeability and trust. But how do you build likeability and trust quickly with people you don't know?

The power of what I share here shouldn't be underestimated. People often *talk* about building trust, but rarely talk about *how* to do it in easy-to-understand, practical terms. When you begin doing these things regularly, you'll see your success rocketing.

The two things that so often scupper our chances of being seen as likeable and trustworthy are nervousness and anxiety at one end of the spectrum, and too much bravado at the other. Neither of these characteristics will help you. In the former case, you may appear hesitant and unsure of what you're doing; in the latter, too much bravado causes your audience's inner BS detectors to go into overdrive, which then erodes trust.

Over the years, we've seen what works, and here we have broken it down so you have a simple plan when talking with agents and landlords. It may look simple, but most people are not doing these things. The two most important things to do in practical terms are to be curious, and to do what you say you will do.

Be curious

Don't overlook the importance of this one tip. It sounds so simple, yet most people don't do it. Adopting curiosity will help to prevent the nerves and bravado that come from anxiety. It's much more difficult to be anxious when your focus is on understanding someone else. When I say 'be curious', you know what to do. You naturally listen more and focus on understanding the other person very well. You'll naturally ask more questions, and when you combine curiosity with the win-

win negotiation skills I will talk about in the next chapter, you'll become a magnet for opportunity.

Do what you say you will do

The second tip is important, too. You show people who you are by what you do, not by what you say. So, remember that with everything you do, you need to do what you say you will do, when you say you will do it. When you do that, you are on the fast track to being seen as likeable and trustworthy. Most people do not do these things; not through malice, but because we are all so worried and preoccupied with ourselves. Stand out from the crowd by doing what you say you'll do.

TOP TIP

Relax

Your goal is *not* to be perfect.

Your goal is to **be curious**.

Your goal is to **do what you say you will**.

Your goal is to **arrange a viewing**, where it makes sense and where the property works for you.

It's easier to relax when your goal is not perfection.

The bottom line is: you're solving a problem for landlords and letting agents by getting more properties let out more quickly with less hassle. You will become the go-to person. Temi found her first deal working with agents even though she is shy and hates the idea of 'selling'. In Temi's Rockstars interview, you'll hear her talk more about this, and it's well worth watching it on the **Rockstar Essentials website**[25].

THE POWER OF YOUR SOCIAL PITCH

You now understand how to work with landlords and agents. The final piece of the Magnetic Marketing puzzle is to tell everyone what you do. We've had deals from our cleaners, our builders, business networking events and more. This approach will work for you, too.

How to get known for something

To be successful in rent to rent, you don't need to be famous; you do need to be known as *the* person for a specific kind of HMO in your location. And it can be a small location. For example, Maria Opaniran got her first three properties through referrals from landlords. Maria provided a great service, involves her young family in her business, and landlords love working with her.

And the way to achieve the same thing is to:

,   Be specific about what you do and how you help.

,   Be consistent about showing people what you do.

It's important because people talk. Many people will take to Facebook and ask for recommendations of a plumber for their house share. Or they'll mention to a friend that they've just bought an HMO. Or they'll complain on Facebook about their HMO letting agent. And when that happens, you want your name to be on people's lips. It's important that people know who you are and what you do. The great thing about this approach is that it's absolutely free.

Tell people about what you do everywhere you go – at work, at your children's school, at business networking events, on holiday, while out walking your dog. People often ask what you do. Have a compelling answer ready.

Actually… it's not quite free. To do this, you have to ditch your comfort zone and start practising your social pitch.

YOUR SOCIAL PITCH

The way to really get up and running is to create your own social pitch. A social pitch is like a business pitch, but for everyone you meet socially. These won't necessarily be property people who know what an HMO is, but people you meet in your day-to-day life through business or work, or family, friends and so on.

What I want you to do is practise it so you can say it in a minute at most – so it absolutely rolls off your tongue and is really easy for you to say. You want to become known as the HMO person in your area (or the house share person, as many people don't know what an HMO is). If one of your friends knows someone who's having a nightmare with their house share, you should be the first person they think of.

As an example, let me give you my one-minute social pitch:

'We transform house shares from hellish to heavenly, and give landlords guaranteed rent, freedom from tenant management and total peace of mind. If you know a house share landlord who'd like to make their house shares hassle-free, let them know that the Property Angels at HMO Heaven can help.'

Yours must suit *you*. Ours is a little cheesy, but it suits us and our personalities.

What to include in your social pitch:

- How you help
- Who you help
- Benefits to the landlord/agent
- A call to action – optional, depending on who you're speaking to.

You can switch the order round to suit you.

Embrace the art of experimentation. You get clarity *after* you do this, not before you start. So if you feel confused about what you offer and what to write, you are right! The clarity comes after you've written it, practised it and received feedback on it. Spending a little time crafting a short pitch that, with practice, will trip off your tongue will significantly boost your confidence, and will bring the deals to you. Be Bolder and let's start sharing what we are up to, and the ways in which we can help landlords and agents.

EXERCISE
Your Social Pitch

Use the **Your Social Pitch Worksheet**, which you can download from the **Rockstar Essentials website**: **rent2rentsuccess.com/essentials**, and let's get started so you can begin confidently telling everybody what you do.

Remember, your social pitch is not an essay or something to be fearful of; it's around 50 words – five lines – that tell someone what you do. You should be able to say it comfortably, without rushing, in about 30 seconds. It's your sizzle, not your steak. It's your elevator pitch, your answer to the question, 'What do you do?'

Remind yourself of your business values

▶ *Action*

Review your earlier work on your business values. It's important to keep them in mind when you're writing your social pitch, as your values are the essence of your business.

Draft your social pitch

▶ *Action*

For 10 minutes, brainstorm the following four questions/statements you should address in your pitch:

1. **How you can help**
2. **Who you help**
3. **Benefits to the landlord/agent**
4. **A call to action – optional, depending on who you're speaking to**

▶ *Action*

Form sentences from the words and phrases you jotted down. You can switch the order around to suit you.

It should reflect your personality, but keep it punchy and concise. Don't use words that tie your tongue, or fancy words, acronyms and 'property speak' – use words everyone can understand. Consider a play on words if it works with your company name and business values. For example, our company name is HMO Heaven, so we talk about transforming our properties from 'hellish to heavenly' and call ourselves Property Angels.

As a guide, remember your finished social pitch will be about 50 words long, and you'll be able to share it comfortably, without rushing, in about 30 seconds. (This is a guide only, to help you write a pitch, not a book.)

Practice your social pitch

▶ *Action*

Practice, practice, practice. Our Kickstarters know the support of the community has been invaluable to them in helping to get their pitch perfect.

- If you're getting tongue-tied – tweak it.
- If it's too long – tweak it.
- If friends still don't understand what you do – tweak it.

▶ *Action*

Hone and finalise your social pitch from the feedback you receive. Aim for a pitch you can say comfortably, without rushing, in about 30–40 seconds.

▶ *Action*

Keep practising!

Share your social pitch with EVERYONE!

▶ *Action*

Share your social pitch. If you don't share it, people won't know what you do. Your confidence will build the more you practise and share.

Your first deal could come from anywhere: a direct-to-landlord letter, an agent, your neighbour, a colleague, the person you chat to every day at the gym. And that is why it is so important to tell everyone you know about what you do.

With your social pitch, the secret is to practise, practise, practise. Once you start practising and getting feedback from people, you'll hone your pitch and see what works. We didn't start out with the pitch above; we had a much longer one, but we found it confused people. Practising is how you'll get really good and feel really comfortable explaining what you do. Within our Rent 2 Rent Kickstarter Programme, one of the things people get incredible confidence from is the chance to hone, craft and practise their pitch in a supportive community. Do ensure you find like-minded people to support you in crafting your pitch and moving from confusion to clarity.

Be OK to play with this.

Be curious about the reactions.

Be open to questions.

If people are negative, don't take it personally. It's not about you; it's about what *they* think is possible. Lean into the questions, ask why they think what they think. It will all be useful information. Don't wait until you feel confident. The confidence will come later. Feel the fear. And do it anyway.

Be Bolder.

BE BOLDER ON SOCIAL MEDIA

It's a natural human tendency to want to hide. To play it safe. It's because we want approval. When we speak out, we have a fear of being judged harshly and ostracised from the group, which for our ancestors could be fatal. For us, it's not – we're not going to die because we posted on Facebook and now our critical colleague or cousin knows about our property business – but it can sometimes feel like it. Push yourself to do things that take you outside your comfort zone. It will probably feel awkward at first, but it will become easier. And it will be worth it.

- Commit to living your life for you, not for your critics (you will always have them).
- Show up for you.
- Be your biggest cheerleader.
- Always be there for you, no matter what.

Think about the people you enjoy watching on Facebook or YouTube. They're human; sometimes they stumble on their words or forget what they were saying. You still think they're great. And it's the same for you. You're getting the essence across; it's not important to say your pitch word for word, exactly as written – after all, nobody except you knows what you wrote. It's important to get across the intentions of your business and the way you help people.

Doing this will attract lots of new business to you.

Remember: it might not happen straight away. It sometimes takes a while, but keep showing everyone how you provide value, how you solve problems for people, and the business will come. Every human wants to solve their problems with the least possible friction. If you become well known as an HMO problem solver, you will find yourself in demand.

SUMMARY OF MAGNETIC MARKETING

In this chapter, we discussed:

- The three best ways to attract landlords and letting agents to you
- How you can deliver what landlords and agents want
- The way to get over any anxieties you have, and quickly build likeability and trust
- The power of your social pitch.

Of course, we haven't been able to cover everything – there just isn't the space in this chapter – but you have good grounding to get started and visit **Rockstar Essentials** for more.

AN IMPORTANT REMINDER

You are enough exactly as you are.

And you will succeed.

Will you be amazing straight out of the gate? Probably not.

But the good news is: you don't have to be.

You will get better.

Just get started!

Magnetic Marketing is a big part of your success. Success is outside your comfort zone. Believe Bigger and Be Bolder are your watchwords for this.

Let's move on now to Make the Deals.

STEP 5
MAKE THE DEALS

Discover how to analyse deals in minutes, negotiate like a ninja and do the deals!

'Negotiate as if your life depends on it.
Because it does.'

Chris Voss

WHAT IS MAKE THE DEALS?

This chapter will explain how to evaluate each property financially and will give you some under-used skills to negotiate like a ninja and agree win-win deals. You may not be ready to put this into action yet, but I want to show you this too, so you have an overview of the process for when the time comes.

WHY IS MAKE THE DEALS IMPORTANT TO RENT 2 RENT SUCCESS?

Numbers don't lie, and knowing your numbers is an important part of any business. This includes rock-solid analysis of deals, including all the costs. Once you know a property will work, imagine what you could do if you were a negotiation ninja; imagine if you had the power of persuasion, helping others to get what they want, whilst also giving you what you want, and having both parties feeling good about it. Negotiation is not about manipulating people or trying to persuade them to do things they don't want to do; it's about presenting an offer in the optimal way for the best chance of acceptance. And, obviously, having offers accepted is crucial to success in rent to rent.

HOW TO MAKE THE DEALS

In this chapter, we'll explore what you need to know, from analysing a proposal to signing on the dotted line for a great deal:

1. **How to work out if a deal is profitable using our Deal Analyser**
2. **Making irresistible offers to landlords**
3. **Making irresistible offers to letting agents**
4. **Three under-used negotiation tips you need to succeed**
5. **Making the deal with the right contracts.**

HOW TO WORK OUT IF A DEAL IS PROFITABLE USING OUR DEAL ANALYSER

The Rent 2 Rent Success Deal Analyser is an essential part of your toolkit. It lets you make sure a property will be profitable before you take it on, instead of worrying and wondering 'Should I do this deal?', 'Is this really a good deal?', 'How much rent can I afford to pay?' Don't guess! Know for sure.

You probably understand in theory how important it is to really understand your numbers before taking on a deal. However, I see so many people just working out figures in their heads before taking on a property. I want to urge you to take five minutes to put the figures into our Deal Analyser and know for sure. Our Deal Analyser gives you total clarity.

It saves you time, money and stress. If you love spreadsheets, you'll really enjoy this! And if you're not a spreadsheet person, I want to reassure you that what I'm going to show you is simple. I wasn't a spreadsheet person, either, but I do love being able to go into the analyser and see exactly the profit we'll make on each property. On the **Rockstar Essentials website rent-2rentsuccess.com/essentials**, you can download the Rent 2 Rent Success Deal Analyser, so you can start using it in your business. This is the same spreadsheet that we use for all our deals. We have honed it after years of experience.

It's simple to use:

- Put in all the rental income by room.
- Put in all the costs line by line.

, Our Deal Analyser will show you how much profit you will make on each property.

This will help you to calculate how much rent you can pay for each property in order to make the profit you would like. Don't let your heart run away with your head. Remember, no deal is better than a bad deal that loses you money. The purpose of the forecast is to overestimate the costs slightly and underestimate the income a little, so you can be certain the deal will be profitable.

What profit should I aim for?

When using our Deal Analyser, you'll notice that you can try out different rents to the landlord or letting agent and immediately see the impact on your profit.

So, how much profit should you be aiming for? As a guide, we suggest you aim for £100 per room per month.

So on a four-bed, that's £400 profit per month.

On a five-bed, it's £500 profit per month.

On a six-bed, it's £600 profit per month.

On a seven-bed, it's £700 profit per month… and so on.

Do I always have to achieve this amount of profit to move forward?

That's up to you, but these are really good figures to aim for. If you had a five-bed deal come in at £480 per month profit and you've negotiated as much as you can, it still might be a great deal to get you started. Don't cut your margins too thinly, though. You need a profit that makes it worthwhile! Within the Kickstarter Community, we'll give you feedback on all your deals, because it's so reassuring to know you're on the right track – or not – before you start.

MAKING IRRESISTIBLE OFFERS TO LANDLORDS

A successful deal starts with an utterly irresistible offer.

Most of what we talk about here is applicable to both landlords and agents. But some things are unique to agents, and I'll add them in the next section. Typically, your offer will be lower than the advertised rent. That is partly because you will be paying the bills, which the landlord would be paying from the advertised rent. You need a way of presenting your offer in a way that answers the question 'why is the rent lower?' and provides a compelling reason to move ahead.

Let me clarify here that often you're not actually offering less than a landlord receives *after* their costs. If a landlord has a property to let for £3,000 and is paying all the bills, the £3,000 is very clear in her mind. The cost of all the bills and what she actually receives after all the bills, voids, and so on is not. So your offer will need to clearly show how it compares with what she's receiving now after all her costs, which may not be so clear in her mind.

In Magnetic Marketing, we talked about how to learn what the real issues are for the property owner and/or agent. With that understanding of what landlords and agents are looking for, you can craft a compelling offer.

In our Irresistible Offer Template we include:

Guaranteed rent

This is what people want to know first. How much rent will they receive?

Explain why

I used to think a landlord wouldn't be interested in *why* I was offering a particular guaranteed rent – surely they would just want to know what the rent was? But I've found that not to be true. Landlords and agents want to understand that your offer is fair. People have an inbuilt instinct about what is fair, and because many landlords and agents don't understand the costs of running an HMO, your offer may seem unfairly low, when it is not.

We need to explain to landlords and agents exactly *why* ours is an amazing deal for them. To do this, you need to *clearly and explicitly* show what's in it for them. This may seem obvious, but I'm surprised by how many offers don't do this. I'm often asked what should be included in offers, so I know this will help you get it right.

This is important, because a landlord or agent is used to thinking about the gross rent before the bills. That might make your rent look too low initially, so we need to educate them.

For example: The landlord or agent is expecting £2,000 for a five-bed property. Your offer is £900.

This is where you explain the difference, which is in what you will do and pay for. Then you want to show how amazing your services are, compared with those of a standard letting agent.

Social proof

As customers, we buy products and services that we know other people have bought, as this gives us confidence. By using social proof, such as testimonials, reviews or trust icons (such as showing your membership of the Property Redress Scheme), you'll help potential customers feel more confident in choosing you.

If you're just starting out, don't dismiss this out of hand. Think creatively about anything you can add that will make working with you feel less risky for the landlord or agent.

We got our first deal without testimonials.

And so did our Rent 2 Rent Rockstars.

And so can you.

Next steps

You want to tell your landlord what the next steps are.

Choose 1-3 bullets, which gives them clarity and certainty about how to work with you.

With offers to landlords sorted, let's move on to agents.

MAKING IRRESISTIBLE OFFERS TO LETTING AGENTS

The information relevant to offers to landlords is also relevant to agents, but with a few additions. Agents are still most keen to have lower risk and to keep their commission. Of course, when making an offer to an agent, you don't want to say anything that is anti-agent!

We're including the same items in our offer, with the addition of the agent fees. We need to ensure it's clear that the agent understands their commission will be paid as normal (if fully managed) and that you'll pay a finder's fee (if tenant find only). See Magnetic Marketing for a reminder of what 'fully managed' and 'tenant find only' mean.

THREE UNDER-USED NEGOTIATION TIPS YOU NEED TO SUCCEED

The best book I know of on the topic of negotiation is *Never Split the Difference – Negotiating as if Your Life Depended on*

It by former FBI hostage negotiator Chris Voss.[26] This book changed my thinking and the outcomes I'm able to achieve, and it could do the same for you.

Tip 1 – reflect back

Voss talks about the concept of mirroring. This is where you repeat the last three words (or the important few words) of what someone has just said. Similarity is so comforting; one study found that waiters got a 70% higher tip when they practised mirroring than when they used positive reinforcement. Mirroring activates empathy and bonding. Mastering this one step will help you learn more than anyone else in any given situation. Knowing more will reveal to you how to pitch your offer more effectively to solve the other person's needs, and these needs are often not what you assume. Work hard *not* to assume.

Tip 2 – point out the problems

Often, landlords or agents may have vague feelings of uncertainty they can't put their finger on, which will stop them from moving forward. Bringing up these 'problems' and talking about them makes the problems seem smaller and less worrying.

Or, as Voss says, 'Don't feel their pain, label it!'

Labelling is a way of acknowledging someone's feelings. Usually, we only do this for people we know well, so it deepens the intimacy between people. The skill is in spotting the feelings or anxieties that are not being discussed.

I must say, I was sceptical about this one and felt self-conscious about 'using' it. I wondered if it was a manipulation. But what I found is it's simple, effective and actually makes you feel more connected to the other person, so it feels good, too. It's something you're using to understand more deeply. It makes your communications more honest. You'd use phrases like:

- 'It seems like you're worried that I won't pay the rent like your previous tenant.'
- 'It looks like you still have some concerns about going ahead.'
- 'It sounds like you're not happy with the rent offer I made.'

Be comfortable allowing silence here for a reply; often people will have to think about why they feel unsure. They may not have fully voiced their concerns before, even to themselves. That's why this is so powerful.

Tip 3 – ask calibrated questions

Once someone answers, delve deeper with more questions so you can fully understand their concerns and their thinking. Ask the right questions; Voss describes calibrated questions where you invite the other person to tell you what the problem is rather than causing conflict by telling them what the problem is.

Here are some examples:

- How can I help make this better?
- How would you like me to proceed?
- How can we solve this problem?

Calibrated questions make the other person feel like they are more listened to and more in control.

MARIA OPANIRAN'S FIRST PROPERTY

It can be hard to imagine how this all works in practice, so now feels like a good time to reintroduce Maria. Maria is a mum of three children aged 11, 14 and 16, and she's a full-time IT project manager in the financial services sector. In Maria's own words, she's a busy woman! She was hesitant before starting, but once Maria joined Kickstarter, she went all in and now has three properties and a fourth in the pipeline.

My hesitation about getting started is that I'm a very quiet person. People told me I'm not, but I think I am, because you have your internal struggles as well, your internal insecurities. I started telling myself I could do it. I just ignored my insecurities. I went for it.

I found a property by contacting letting agents and the viewing was with the landlord. The landlord just said to me

> 'Look, I'm moving to the US and I want someone I can trust to look after my property.' That's exactly what she said to me. I think she just felt from our little conversation that she could trust me with her property.
>
> I think basically, because of the way I am, she fell in love with me. Let me use that word because it just felt that way. Her previous tenant vandalised the property so she was sceptical at first, but I think she just knew that I would not be like that. She was concerned that I was going to look after her property, but she liked the fact that I was going to pay guaranteed rent.'

You can see Maria tell her story in her own words on our **Rockstar Essentials website**[27]. Most people find that landlord motivation is so much simpler than they thought, and they often repeat the saying 'people buy people', because it's so true. Maria also got a lease option on the property, which means she can buy it over time without needing a big deposit or a mortgage.

Our exchange with delayed completion story

Our negotiation skills were important when we negotiated the 'exchange with delayed completion' property we talked about in Model Magic. We assumed the seller would want a monthly payment of around £1,000. Luckily, we knew not to assume and asked them instead – and they actually wanted £320 per month. In that way, we were able to perfectly meet their wants and our own, simply by listening carefully and asking questions. Ask. Don't assume.

A FEW FINAL THOUGHTS

Simplicity is your friend. Our brains do not like confusion. We don't like having to work things out – it takes too much energy – and, as the well-known marketing saying goes, 'a confused mind never buys'. There are a lot of different ways to structure a deal. We find it's best to offer the landlord or agent two ways based on the information you've learned from them and what their wants and needs are.

Leave the door open. We've had a number of occasions where landlords originally turned us down, saying our offer was too low, and came back years later after really looking at their costs and seeing that our rent was actually better than what they were receiving after paying all the costs!

Follow up. It's so, so important to follow up on all your landlords and agents. Use a system that helps you do that.

There's no need to wait until you're negotiating your first rent to rent property to begin improving your skills. Try implementing some of these strategies when negotiating simple things such as household chores. Roleplay rent to rent scenarios, too. We've noticed in Kickstarter that it makes a huge difference. Roleplaying helps you settle your mind and build confidence; it shows you what you know, and that you can share much more than you thought.

Let's move on now to making the deal with the right contracts.

MAKING THE DEAL WITH THE RIGHT CONTRACTS

You've found a great property, negotiated and agreed a deal, and now it's time to formally Make the Deal.

You're ready to sign on the dotted line for your first deal. But, for many people, signing their first deal is confusing and worrying. They're unsure which contract to use. When you'll be investing time and money, you want to know that your investment is protected.

So, let's get down to the business of contracts.

Important reminder:

I am not a solicitor, and this is not legal advice. I am simply talking here from my own experience of England and Wales. It's important to do your own due diligence and check the legalities in your area.

In this section, we walk you through what you need to know about rent to rent contracts. There are two types of rent to rent contracts that should be used between you as the rent to renter and a landlord or letting agent.

- Lease agreement
- Management agreement

Lease agreement

This agreement is a commercial lease and gives you the right to rent the property and rent it out to your own tenants or guests for a specified period of time.

You would use a rent to rent lease agreement when:

, Your agreement is directly with the owner

AND

, The property is an existing HMO or commercial property

OR

, The property is unencumbered (has no mortgage).

Management agreement

This agreement gives you the right to manage the property on a specified basis (e.g. HMO or serviced apartment).

You would use a rent to rent management agreement when:

, Your agreement is with the letting agent or the owner

AND

, The property is not an existing HMO or commercial property.

Don't use an AST or a company let agreement!

Use a lease agreement or a management agreement. ASTs (Assured Shorthold Tenancy agreements) and company let agreements are *not* the right contract between you and the landlord or letting agent. ASTs are used between you and the tenant, and company let agreements give you the right to manage the property where your tenants are employees of your company.

TOP TIP

Ensure you do this!

With either a lease or a management contract, it is important to ensure you explain to the property owner that they must check that their mortgage lender (if there is a mortgage) and insurer will allow use of the property as a house share (HMO) for the type of tenant you want.

The simple solution to this is to work with properties that are already HMOs, because the owners should already have the right borrowing and insurance in place.

Do I need a solicitor?

You can go to a solicitor and have your contract drawn up, but using a solicitor can be expensive and time-consuming. You might think that you'll get a better result and you'll be more protected if anything goes wrong.

We thought that, too.

We were surprised to find that many solicitors do not understand the business model of rent to rent, even though they say they do! And if you have any issues and go back to them, you will find that, in the 'engagement of services' contract you signed, you agreed that they are *not* liable if anything goes wrong (with extremely rare exceptions). They are solicitors, after all, and they use the law to protect themselves, too.

To protect yourself as much as possible, it's important to use the right contract and include the right clauses. Many people don't realise that solicitors start with a template for each contract type and then rely on *you* to advise all the clauses you would like to see added, and the ones you need removed. When you're starting out, you won't know all the clauses you need, and if they are unfamiliar with rent to rent (as most solicitors are), your solicitor won't know which specific clauses you need either.

Over the years, we've had our contract reviewed and revised to add new clauses. For example, we've had a 'coronavirus clause' added, so that if anything like coronavirus happens again, we will have a provision in the contract to enable us to renegotiate the guaranteed rent.

Another example is having a break clause, something we mentioned in Mythbusters. We have a one-way break clause. This gives us the ability to end the contract in a specified number of months agreed with our landlords. The mistake I see many new entrants making is agreeing two-way break clauses; you don't want to have landlords or agents able to exit early if you are meeting your contractual obligations. This is especially important if you have invested in the property and need time to recoup your investment.

Another example of a contract mistake I often see people struggling with is lack of clauses about repairs; for example, if a landlord refuses to make essential repairs, such as fixing a broken boiler in the winter. Our contract states that owners must respond to emergency repairs in a specified period and agree any works to be carried out. If this doesn't happen, we are able to carry out the works, recovering the funds from the rent. We've never had to do this, because we have great relationships with all of our landlords, but the clause is there for exceptional cases to protect our housemates.

We also include a clause stating that if any legal or statutory changes impact our ability to multi-let the property, we can renegotiate and/or exit the agreement.

These are just some of many important examples I could give you about clauses to be included in your rent to rent contract.

Having the right contract is crucial. Although it's an investment, the cost of the right contracts is much less than the cost of legal disputes. And that's not just the financial cost – it's your time and emotional energy, which are much more precious. Get the right contracts.

Do I need to go to a solicitor for every new rent to rent property I take on?

Now, this might be controversial, but my answer is *No, you don't!* Do letting agents go to a solicitor for a new contract each time they take on the management of a new property? No, they don't. They edit the existing contract with the details for the specific owner, property and agreement.

Exception

The only exception to this is where you are taking a property on rent to rent with an option to buy. This is where you are contracting with a property owner to rent and then buy their property, using either a lease option or an exchange with delayed completion, or another strategy. In these instances, it is essential to have a bespoke agreement drawn up or reviewed by a solicitor for each property.

An important reminder

Contracts are the backdrop.

In rent to rent, property, business and good relationships thrive if they are win-win.

It's good for you and it's good for us.

It's good for our landlords and it's good for us.

It's good for our housemates and it's good for us.

Enter every agreement and new relationship in the spirit of win-win.

 Your contracts are there as a safety net, not a first point of call. You want to exit using the lift, not by jumping out of a window and hoping for the best.

We all know litigation is expensive in terms of money, time, and emotional energy. Having the right contracts in place will mean you are less likely to have to do it.

We've made our rent to rent contracts available because we saw so many people using expensive solicitors who didn't have the expertise to deliver what is needed for a rent to rent business. But we haven't just included the contracts; we've also included a guide to when to use each contract, and an explainer document explaining each clause and translating the Legalese to English. It's a sample completed document so you can see what goes where, and a template Word document you can edit and start using straight away.

SUMMARY OF MAKE THE DEALS

In this chapter, we discussed all the steps to go from 'potential property' to 'signed on the dotted line':

- How to work out if a deal is profitable using our Deal Analyser
- Making irresistible offers to landlords
- Making irresistible offers to letting agents
- Three under-used negotiation tips you need to succeed
- Making the deal with the right contracts

Let's move on to Manage and Multiply your success!

STEP 6

MANAGE AND MULTIPLY

Understand how to manage and systemise your business, for the freedom you want as your business grows.

'All you need to do is begin living your life as if it were important. To take your life seriously. To create it intentionally. To actively make your life into the life you wish it to be.'

— Michael E Gerber

WHAT IS MANAGE AND MULTIPLY?

This chapter is all about making a house into a home, turning a property into profit… and then multiplying it. You might feel more comfortable with turning a house into a home than turning a property into profit; one feels like a noble endeavour, and the other doesn't. Be reassured, though, that what we'll discuss here are the steps to having a business you feel proud of that delivers for your landlords, your housemates and you.

Even though you may not be at this stage yet, I'm setting out all six steps in the Rent 2 Rent Success System, so it's here when you need it.

WHY IS MANAGE AND MULTIPLY IMPORTANT FOR RENT 2 RENT SUCCESS?

This is important because it's the final piece in the puzzle, but it's the section where people can easily get lost. We find that people who already have rent to rent properties are joining our Kickstarter Programme simply because their business doesn't feel like freedom. They feel overwhelmed and in chaos. That's not what rent to rent success feels like. They want to put in place simple systems to make their business run easily, as though it were on tracks. It's actually easier to run a good HMO than a disorganised one. Here we show you how to set yourself up for success in a way that most people don't.

HOW DO YOU MANAGE AND MULTIPLY?

What we're going to cover in this chapter is how to:

1. **Make your HMOs heavenly**
2. **Find and onboard great tenants**
3. **Manage your property**
4. **Multiply your success.**

MAKE YOUR HMOS HEAVENLY

Here we bring you simple ways to make your HMO heavenly with all the processes we've learned from HMO Heaven, our award-winning HMO management agency in Newport, alongside the hundreds of people we've worked with.

Breathe deeply… and relax.

I say this because lots of people I talk to are terrified about refurbishment. And as we said earlier, your thoughts create your feelings, actions and results. If you think negative thoughts about the refurb, it can leave you feeling anxious. If *you* feel hesitant about this step, I want you to consciously remind yourself that lots of other people have done this – and you can, too.

Not every property will need a refurbishment; you'll sometimes take on a property where all you need is a bit of dressing.

I'll walk you through the process.

Before

Before you pick up the keys, you'll have an idea of what needs to be done. The ideal is to plan in advance and start any works on the day you pick up the keys.

Photos

Before starting, though, take 'before' photos. These are helpful for your before and after photos, which will become business assets for you.

General planning

How far do you want to go? Do you want a basic homely finish or a more high-end finish?

When considering this, think about:

- The rents you can get in your area
- The property market in your area
- The type of tenant you want to attract
- The rent you want to achieve
- The amount you want to spend on the refurb (as you calculated in our Deal Analyser).

Consider this important question:

What do I need to do to be able to let a property consistently at the rent I want, and to have it be a lovely home for the types of housemates I would like to attract?

Refurbishment planning

Create a list of everything that needs to be done and allocate a person, budget and time period for each. A spreadsheet is a good way to do this. When you've done it a few times, it'll give you a refurb checklist. Go through that line by line and allocate a cost and a person to each line. What's the plumber going to do? What's the electrician going to do? What's the decorator going to do? Also write down what you're going to do and when; you'll need to work out when you need your dressing to arrive, when you need your furniture to arrive, and so on.

During

Stay on top

As you implement your plan, stay on top of things. Make sure that things are progressing the way you want them to. Be on-site regularly, or ask a trusted person to visit. If anything is going wrong, it's better to know sooner rather than later. Whatever happens, breathe deeply and remind yourself that you can do this. In a short time, you will have the cashflow and be well on your way. People will be asking you how you did it.

After

Photos

Having professional photos will be important for selling your rooms and showcasing what you do to landlords and agents.

These will be your photos for marketing the rooms; we even do short videos of each room that we can send to people interested in the property.

Review

Look at what went well and what didn't, and make a note so that your next refurb is even better.

REAL LIFE REFURBS

To make this more real for you, here are two examples.

Our refurbishment

This is one of our properties, and we spent £6,400 on it. We included/budgeted for this in our Deal Analyser ahead of making the deal, so we were clear what our profits would be and knew we were happy with them. Our monthly profit after all costs, including the refurbishment, is £615.

The five-year profit for this contract is £37,000, after all costs, including voids. This is a great investment. Where else could you invest £6,400 and get your money back plus an additional £37,000 within five years?

Having said that, most of the people we work with are spending under £3,000 on refurbishments – and we also spend much less than we used to. We now understand how to get great results spending less money. I chose this higher cost example to show you that even when you spend more, a property can still work very well.

This property was already furnished with Ikea furniture, and we kept that furniture. There was a major issue with damp in the lower ground floor lounge, and the landlord there wanted to just paint over it. But we knew that, although it would look better for a few months, this wouldn't solve the problem; the damp would have been back within months, creating an uncomfortable home for our housemates. We encouraged the landlord to pay for it to be cleaned up, treated and repainted. It's much better to do this while the property is empty at the start. She appreciated the nudge, as the house had been plagued by damp for many years, creating voids, stress and worry. The landlord paid for that.

It had been decorated in the last few years, but it was still a bit grubby, so we decorated throughout to make it lovelier for our housemates. It makes our job much easier in selling the rooms going forwards. Whatever decisions need to be made, we look for an ethical option that's a win-win. We find in the longer term that it is better for business, too.

Photo: Before Refurbishment

Photo: After Refurbishment

MARK FITZGERALD'S STORY

Mark is based in South Yorkshire and has nine properties now, with three more in the pipeline. You'll see in the photos below that Mark's properties look great, yet he spends a modest amount on them.

'I was very lucky with my first deal, because it had been newly refurbished about three months before I took it on, so I didn't actually have to do anything. It was a real case of walking into it. I had a modest pot of money from my redundancy and I was living on that. So, I knew I couldn't burn straight through that with refurbs. I looked at a lot of properties before I got my first deal, and some needed £10K spending on them for new kitchens and bathrooms to bring them up to a decent level. I wasn't willing to put that sort of money into it.'

Many people are choosing to stick to properties requiring little refurbishment and being very successful. You can do that, too.

Keeping your refurb costs down

Firstly, always negotiate with the owner. Owners expect to pay for the upgrading of their properties and are often willing to pay for the work needed. Here are other ways to keep your costs lower.

Only take on properties in good condition

People sometimes worry that they'll end up paying too much for refurbishment. Remember, it's all within your control. If you view a property that's a good deal but it costs more than you want to spend, you don't have to take it on. You could ask the landlord to do the refurb, do a joint venture with someone else who can fund the project, or sell it on to someone else and earn some money at the same time! We see that happening often within the Kickstarter Community.

DIY

Work with family and friends and get the property looking ship-shape yourselves; in any refurb, contractor labour is usually one of your biggest costs. When you can do those things yourself, you save a lot of money.

As you've seen in the examples above, you really don't have to spend a fortune to get a great result for your housemates.

Let's move on now to furniture.

Furniture

Your property is looking good after the refurbishment, if it needed one. Now it's time to furnish your property. Furniture can be expensive, so I wanted to explain the main way to keep your costs down.

New furniture – buying outright

This is what we do, as for us it's the most cost- and time-efficient way to do things. For example, in the first six months of 2019, we onboarded six properties, but we chose not to commit the time to buying second-hand as it's much more time-intensive. If you have more time and less money, though, read on to the following sections; you can save a lot of money by *not* buying new furniture.

Upcycling furniture

If you have ugly furniture in the property, you could upcycle it with a lick of paint, so long as it's sturdy. This is time-consuming but will save you money.

Buying second-hand furniture

I know people have massive success with this and really manage to keep their furniture costs to a minimum. So, if that's your forte and you can invest the time to source second-hand furniture, then it's a great way to keep your costs down. Facebook marketplace, Gumtree and eBay are great places to start. And anyvan.com can be useful and cost-effective for delivery.

Renting furniture

Renting your furniture will normally cost more over time than buying new furniture but, on the upside, you don't have big upfront costs. You just pay for your furniture each month out of your cashflow. We have added some links to furniture leasing companies in our furniture list on the **Rockstar Essentials website**.

Dressing and photography

Dressing

We use a simple system for dressing which includes adding homely touches to the property. Sometimes people tell me they feel overwhelmed by the prospect of dressing, so if that's you, I'd like to give you three reminders:

- The goal is for it to be 'easy to rent' not 'ready for a feature in Homes & Gardens'.
- Do the best you can with what you have.
- Your first property won't be your best. Be OK with that!

Do I really need a professional photographer?

Photos are *hugely important* in renting your rooms.

Most potential housemates will find you online. The quality of your photos will determine whether they ever click on your ad and arrange a viewing. To have people queueing up for your rooms, you need great photos. There is no way around this. So, ideally, yes: use a professional photographer. When you dress your property for the first time, that is the time to get your professional photos. It's also worthwhile getting a short video of each room.

Unless you know what you're doing with property photography, lighting and composition, I strongly suggest you ask a professional photographer (or at least someone who does photography as a hobby, has an amazing camera and really understands how to create a great photo). The price will vary according to location. People we've spoken to are paying between £50 and £150 per property. This is great value when you think that these are the photos that will be selling your rooms for the next few years. The cost of empty rooms would be much higher.

Photo: Amateur Photo

Photo: Professional Photo

So, we've completed the refurb, dressing and photography. Now let's talk about getting great tenants.

FIND AND ONBOARD GREAT TENANTS

One of the biggest concerns people have when thinking about rent to rent is 'What if I can't rent the rooms?' By following a proven process, choosing the right area and analysing the deal so you know it will be profitable, you are on the way to success. It's also worth saying that you can take on properties that already have tenants, as Loise did – and as we often do, too. When you do need to find great tenants, here's how to do it.

When to advertise your rooms

It's important to start early. Start planning this as soon as you get the keys, if not before. You can start advertising straight away by using a photo from a similar house on your ad. Another way is to complete the best bedroom first. Dress that bedroom. Get the photos online. With this strategy, you can start your viewings earlier, before the rest of the house is completely ready. With a dressed bedroom, an unfinished rest of the house isn't an issue – you'd be surprised how easily rooms sell. Most viewers see moving into a newly refurbished building as a massive plus and are delighted to be able to get in early.

These techniques ensure you can go through referencing, accepting deposits and advance rent, and signing tenancy agreements while you are completing the refurb, so your tenants can move in as soon as the work is finished.

Where to advertise your rooms

SpareRoom – *the* best way to advertise an HMO room in the UK is on SpareRoom. This is a must-do.

In this book, we're focusing on the most effective ways to do things – the 20% of actions that deliver 80% of the results. But there are many other online alternatives, including:

OpenRent – this platform is for landlords, not high street agents. If you try OpenRent, you must upgrade so that your property is on Rightmove and other portals, including Zoopla,

Gumtree and Prime Location. Without the upgrade, there is little benefit as not enough potential tenants visit the Open-Rent website, whereas most are on Rightmove and Zoopla.

Facebook – this is an avenue some people are finding great success with, but it can be location dependent. In some areas, people were finding that the enquiries that came through Facebook were from tenants who were not a good fit for their properties. We've found it's changed over time, and we are now getting a lot of interest from professional tenants. It's worth testing to see whether it works for you. You can try a mix of Facebook marketplace, Facebook groups and even your personal profile.

Other online portals – there are a number of other room websites, such as Easy Roommate. Our experience has been that these are not a worthwhile investment of time because SpareRoom has so much of the traffic, but again you should test your market.

Longer-term local – as well as the online portals, in the longer term you should see which companies your tenants are coming from, and which companies are hiring in the area. Are there developments in the area? Build relationships with HR people at those companies.

THE most important thing about your ad

You might know what I'm going to say here. The most import-ant thing is your first photo. Your lead photo is what will determine whether someone clicks over to your ad. Make sure you have good photos by taking the steps we discussed earlier.

The second and third most important things about your ad are your title and your advert text.

Title – include things that people are most looking for, such as 'Gorgeous Room in Nottingham with HUGE en suite'.

Text – in the ad itself, here are a few things to remember:

- Sell the experience and how good it will feel living there.
- Use positive and welcoming words.
- Include a bullet point list of all the things that are included.
- Include a reason to move quickly.

How to arrange viewings so you have a waiting list

It's not only about your advertising. How you do your viewings is important, as well.

Before the viewing

To avoid wasting your time, ensure that the viewer meets any criteria you have and that you have their contact details *before* organising the viewing.

Booking a viewing

We batch viewings in 15-minute intervals. We do this for a number of reasons:

,   It creates scarcity.

,   It uses our time more efficiently.

,   It gives each person dedicated time with us, which isn't always possible on group viewings.

Video viewings

We offer video viewings for people who can't get to Newport during the week, and this works really well. If you want to do this, get your professional photographer to create a short video for each room when you get your 'after' photos taken.

At the viewing

Listen to your gut – when you're showing your property, listen a lot and take note of who your potential tenant is. Are they friendly and polite, or rude and disinterested? If you get a bad feeling about them and you can't put your finger on it, trust your gut. Your gut is working off a lifetime of experience. You will have a relationship with the person for at least six months, so make sure you're happy with them.

Put your best foot forward – remember to showcase the property by highlighting:

,   The best features of the property – e.g. large lounge, great en suite, big garden

,   The location – e.g. proximity to shops, their office, city centre

,   Your professional housemates – friendliness

- All the things you offer, including all the bills and a professional cleaning service every fortnight
- High-speed internet – so long as it is!

Ask – sometimes, we're so scared of rejection that we don't ask. It's important to get into the habit of asking every viewer whether they'd like to take the room. It's human nature to put off making decisions, so ensure your potential housemates know that the room could go to someone else if they don't act quickly.

Next steps

Have a very simple process for people to reserve a room. Our process involves two simple steps: completing a short reservation form and making a reservation payment. The payment is deducted from the advance rent payable before the tenant moves in. It's allowable under the Tenant Fees Act 2019.

Follow up

Then, follow up. If they don't come back to you, it's worth just a call, or text. Our assistant property manager has had some success with that, because sometimes people are just busy and they don't get round to these things.

We've covered the process up to a tenant reserving a room. Now, let's go on to how to reference your tenants quickly so can be sure you're choosing the right people.

Photo: Our Team - Stephanie, Luke and Nicky

Referencing your potential tenants

Referencing your potential tenants well and doing right to rent checks will save you lots of problems later on.

We use an online Tenant Information Form (TIF), which is supplemented by an employer reference and a landlord reference. This is an automated, all-online form. When a Reservation Form (RF) is completed, the TIF is sent automatically. And when the TIF is submitted, the employer and landlord reference requests are sent automatically. This system is so efficient that sometimes by the time our Assistant Property Manager arrives at his desk, the RF, TIF and references have all been submitted.

If you prefer to outsource this aspect, we have recommendations on our **Rockstar Essentials website.**

Onboarding your tenants

After you have taken care to choose the right tenant, there are some steps to take to ensure you onboard them legally and in a way that shows you care about them and their home.

Contract

Both you and your tenant will sign the Assured Shorthold Tenancy contract. Having the right contract in place with the tenant is as important as having the right contract with the landlord. It is important because it has clauses that are specific to shared houses. If things go wrong, you need to be sure about your contract.

Register deposit

By law, you must register tenant deposits within a government-approved scheme and provide the tenant with the Deposit Prescribed Information within 30 days of receipt. You need a process in place to ensure this is done. We have our housemates confirm they've received it as part of the online Check-in Checklist process we created.

Deposit protection schemes offer two services: a custodial scheme and an insurance scheme. Under a custodial scheme, the money is held by the scheme provider, not by you. This is a free service. Under an insured scheme, you can keep the money in your own bank account during the tenancy, but there is a fee for this service. If you use an insured scheme and retain the tenant's deposit, then the Client Money Protection we discussed in Mind Your Business does apply and the deposits should be held in a 'client money' bank account that's separate from your business bank account.

Inventory

An inventory is your record of the room as it is before a tenant moves in. Having a good one helps prevent deposit disputes, but creating inventories can be very time-consuming. It used to involve lots of photographs and time writing a report. For us as HMO managers, the damage to a room is usually pretty small: the occasional stained mattress or other minor damage. As the risk level is low, we want an inventory process that is quick, inexpensive and accurate, rather than costly and burdensome.

Since we implemented this process, we haven't had a single deposit dispute across hundreds of tenancies. On occasion, a tenant might disagree with something we say in an email, but we only need send a link to the 'before' and 'after' video for the tenant to agree to the deduction. It's that simple, and it's impossible to argue with – and that's a good thing, because disputes with your deposit protection scheme require a lot of time and paperwork and the schemes have a reputation for siding with tenants. A video is a time-efficient way to get a detailed record of the room so that, if you do need to make any deductions for damage, you're ready with your evidence.

Check-in

This section will save you more time and money than you can imagine. The list of items we now include has been honed over hundreds of tenancies and a few years.

A few years ago, we had a more relaxed approach to new housemate check-ins. We didn't always stick to the hard-copy list of things to go through. We didn't always do an in-person check-in if tenants moved in outside of office hours. We found that little problems started cropping up, even though we provided our Household Guide to all our tenants, making it available online through their phone; the reality is that most people don't read it. What we realised was that we needed to go over all the basics in person at check-in. We find this really works well. The 30 minutes we spend with each new housemate save us countless hours later on.

Here are some of the things we cover:

- Logging in to our app
- How to register a maintenance issue on the app, and what qualifies as an emergency
- Recycling – and fees for any additional rubbish collections
- Cleaning – what the cleaners do and don't do
- Deposit Prescribed Information etc., and signature
- Inventory – our Check-in Checklist is completed in person through an online form and the housemate signs to agree it's been completed and understood. It's one of many simple systems we've introduced that really works.

, How to rent guide (in England)
, Certificates – gas safety, energy performance certificate.

MANAGE YOUR PROPERTY

These final steps in the process are to put the pieces in place that will give you the foundations for time freedom as well as financial freedom.

If you hear people saying their HMOs are very time-consuming, it's likely that they don't have the systems in place to help things run smoothly. The benefit of systemising is that it's so much easier to outsource tasks when you're ready to do so. One of the reasons we go into property is to give ourselves more time, not to give ourselves another job. Taking the time to put the right systems in place at the start will save both your time and your sanity later on! Our systems have been honed over years and have allowed us to hire an in-house team and maintain high service levels.

If you bought single lets, you'd have much less management to do – but much less cashflow. With HMOs, you get so much more. You can easily replace the average UK salary with three to five HMOs. So why doesn't everyone do this? Because, well… money and management. Most people think you need a lot of money to do this. Now you realise that isn't true. But yes, HMOs require more management than single lets. And that is what puts a lot of people off getting started. Knowing how to do it well without it taking much time is what we excel in and will share with you now.

Here we're going to give you an understanding of the big wins and the best places to start.

Let's start off with the overriding principle.

A place for everything, and everything in its place

And that place is in the cloud.

It makes sense that all your property documents should be stored in the cloud where you, or any of your team, can access them on any device from anywhere in the world. This will be the foundation of your success, but I'm often surprised by how few people do it. If some of your end-of-tenancy notifications are on WhatsApp, some inventory approvals are in your email, some gas certificates are in your kitchen drawer, and some video inventories are in the photos app on your mobile, you won't get very far! Management will feel very heavy and draining. Messiness like this will give you constant low-level stress when you think about your business. This is the kind of stress that, if left long-term, can be very damaging to your mental and physical health.

Bookkeeping and accounts

Set in place a process for tracking all the income and expenses for your business. You can do this very simply by recording in a spreadsheet, but a more efficient way is to use an accounting software. We have included our recommendations in our **Rockstar Essentials**; this will give you reporting on each property and much more.

Property management software

You have two options in property management. You can use a spreadsheet to track everything or a property management software system.

Spreadsheet

The main pro is that it's free. The main con is that's it's more difficult to use and outsource. Do what you feel is best for you. A spreadsheet keeps costs really low for your first one, but it will take a little more of your time to manage.

Property management software

We use a property management software system. It makes our life so much easier. We can see at a glance how many rooms we have let or are becoming available, and how many tenants have paid their rent. However, perhaps you're a spreadsheet wizard and you can do all this on your spreadsheet, too.

Where a property management system can really come into its own is in your relations with your tenants, contractors and landlords. All maintenance requests are in one place. All property documents are accessible to tenants or assigned to contractors. We can easily message all tenants, a single tenant, a single property, our contractors, or our landlords. And best of all: it's easily outsourceable.

It comes with its own training videos, so when you outsource your tenant onboarding to a virtual assistant you don't have to produce the training materials – it's all there for you. We have our recommended software, some offers, discounts and bonuses on our **Rockstar Essentials website** at **rent2rent-success.com/essentials**. You can choose the option that suits you best.

When you first get started, you'll also need a few other basic processes in place.

Why WhatsApp could ruin your life

I say WhatsApp, but I'm including any kind of instant messaging. Of course, you will need a way to communicate with your tenants. Instant messaging is *not* the way to do it. You are much more likely to be involved in all sorts of bad-tempered minutiae that you shouldn't be involved in! We humans love convenience; if you're on WhatsApp, your housemates will find it so much easier to ask you a question rather than going downstairs to look at something themselves. It's human nature.

The main reason I'm against using a WhatsApp group to correspond with your tenants is that it gives an expectation of an instant reply. People can see whether you've read the message, and it's just a little bit too 24/7. Over time, being constantly 'on call' will erode your mental well-being. Most letting agents are available nine to five and I suggest that, unless there's an emergency, you aim for that too. Keep your sanity, your hair and your good looks!

To help with this, have another way to keep in touch with our tenants. We keep all communications within our property management app, meaning it's all auditable and trackable. We respond to requests daily and will do so at one time, not immediately as they come in (unless they are emergencies).

100% of our housemates use it. It's a benefit of doing the in-person check-in combined with the online Check-in Checklist, which are both completed at the same time. During this process, we actually ask that any housemates who haven't logged in to our property management app do so there and then. We can confirm they have access to all the required documents and inventory, and that they know how to log any maintenance issues. Most importantly, they understand why logging maintenance within the property management app is important in getting things done more quickly. We explain that we have targets on responding to requests on the property management app. All the team have access to it and, unlike with a personal text, where someone might be on holiday or forget, on our property management app everything is logged, dated and time stamped, and the clock starts ticking. In short, it's better for housemates and it's better for us.

Maintenance

You'll need to let tenants know how to let you know about maintenance issues. We do this by asking the tenant to log maintenance issues on our online property management system. That way everything is date-stamped and nothing gets lost. Our assistant property manager can see all maintenance jobs by property. Tenants are automatically updated in the system about progress on maintenance, so it saves time too. And because all tenants can see when one person has logged a call, we don't then get five messages for each job.

Emergencies

You need a plan for emergencies that covers outside of office hours. There are lots of ways to do this; you could outsource it to a handyman, for example.

We give the tenants a landline telephone number that diverts to an on-call person. This is useful because the number divert can be changed to whoever we want without changing the number that the tenants need to ring. That's been working really well for us. Because of the Check-in Checklist we use with the tenants when they move in, we've defined for them what is an emergency and what isn't, so we get very few calls out of hours now.

You just need to work out what your system is going to be and let your tenants know.

Lock-outs

You will have lock-outs, and some of them will be at very unsocial hours! Our system is that we have key safes for all the properties, so if anybody gets locked out, we can give them the key code for their property and get them back into their home without leaving our office, which is nice. The main thing is to make it outsourceable, so that you don't always have to do it. I know some people do outsource this to an answering service and give them the key codes.

Cleaners

This really does help and is worth the expense. Your cleaners are also your eyes and ears in your properties, noticing any maintenance issues early and helping to keep everything running smoothly. We all know that a house that is not cleaned gets dirty quickly. Skimping on cleaning is a false economy; as cleanliness reduces, so does the quality of the tenants you will attract.

Now you've learned the basics to get started with your property, and the simple systems that you need to make your property work for you. Next, I'll talk about multiplying your success.

Top Tip

Be a great landlord

What does that mean?

It means you provide an excellent service to your tenants: a comfortable, clean, warm and safe place to live, with great service. Just add care.

This is the foundation and framework you will develop as you move forward.

MULTIPLY YOUR SUCCESS

You can repeat the Rent 2 Rent Success System as many times as you'd like. Ensure, though, that what you do works for you.

We discussed in the introduction that our first five properties gave us cashflow after costs of over £3,500 every month, over £43,500 every year, and over £218,000 every five years. *Your* rent to rent success could be three average properties and £1,700 after costs each month, £20,000 each year and over £100,000 every 5 years. You might want to stay in your job and put all the cashflow into investments. Or you might not. I say this to remind you of the importance of *consciously choosing* what success means for you.

 What do you want for your Future You? Don't be derailed by other people's dreams; bring your own into focus and stay focused on *your* path.

Goals help you to evolve and Believe Bigger, Be Bolder and Be a Gamechanger. Remember your gamechanger and toddler brains that we talked about in Mindset Mastery?

Goals keep you in action. They give your gamechanger brain focus and direction and will help you to keep working through the obstacles, emotions and negative thoughts that your toddler brain puts in your way.

Remember: your toddler brain will be working hard to distract you, and this will sometimes be challenging. Your toddler brain does not like new things. This is 100% normal, but being aware of it will help you to recognise when your toddler brain starts to complain and tells you your goals are unachievable. Because you also know about your gamechanger brain, you will be able to use your goals to keep focused and push through towards your dreams and desires with your gamechanger thinking.

EXERCISE
Set Your Goals

Let's develop an action plan to bring your Future You into being, enabling you to hit the five-year goals you identified in Mindset Mastery.

You can download our **Set Your Goals Worksheet** from the **Rockstar Essentials website** at **rent2rentsuccess.com/essentials**

Write your goals

▶ *Action*

Review your earlier work on Future You – what were your deepest desires? What are your desires for your new property business?

- When do I want my business set up completed?
- When do I want my first/next deal?
- How much cashflow do I need for my Future You life?

▶ *Action*

Write your goals in the first person, in the present tense, and be as specific as possible. Include a time frame, dates, amounts, as much detail as you can. For example:

- I am going to get my first deal from a landlord by 7 June 2021. It will be in Bath and generate at least £500 net cashflow a month.

Beware of your toddler

Your toddler brain will likely be going crazy at this point, throwing obstacles and negative thoughts in your way, thinking it's trying to help you, when actually it's just keeping you further away from your desires. It will be asking:

, How am I going to do that?
, That's not possible!
, Who am I trying to kid?
, I should wait – now is not a good time.

Don't worry about the 'how' at this point. Just get your true, unedited goals and desires written down. Having them written means you can read and focus on them every single day.

▶ *Action*

Remind yourself what we talked about in 'Think like a Gamechanger' in Mindset Mastery and the three important thoughts we introduced:

1. **I am always there for me, no matter what.**
2. **I am resourceful.**
3. **I am unstoppable**

▶ *Action*

Write down your action plan.

Write down the actions you would take if you knew you couldn't fail. Write down at least one thing you can do right now to bring you a step closer to where you want to be.

Finalise your goals

▶ *Action*

Finalise your goals. Remember:

- Write them down. You need to be able to read them every day.
- Write them in the first person and in present tense.
- Make them as specific as possible; include a time frame, date and as much detail as possible.

Celebrate your successes

▶ *Action*

Celebrate EVERYTHING!

Often, we only celebrate the milestone events, the big stuff, getting the deal. I'd like you to celebrate everything. The deal won't become a reality without the hundreds/thousands of smaller steps you will need to take along the way, often battling your mighty toddler brain and others.

Reward yourself. Recognise your progress by celebrating every single step.

SUMMARY OF MANAGE AND MULTIPLY

In this chapter, we've covered a lot of ground:

- How to make your HMOs heavenly and the importance of starting where you are, with what you have, and doing what you can step by step.

- How to find and onboard great tenants using a simple step by step process. We've highlighted the importance of good communication and a rock-solid check-in process.

- How to manage your properties moving forward in a way that feels good for you and supports your long-term mental and physical health while giving your housemates a great experience.

- The importance of being a great landlord too and setting your intention.

- Finally, we covered the need to bring your deep desire for your future self into focus. So many of us don't do this. But it brings us joy to arrive at the place where, deep in our heart, we know we're meant to be.

And now is when the magic happens...

PART 3

RENT
2
RENT

BEYOND WORDS: THE JOY (AND TERROR) IN TURNING YOUR COMMITMENTS INTO ACTIONS

One Day or Day One. You decide.

"IF YOU'RE GOING TO QUIT ANYTHING,
QUIT MAKING EXCUSES AND QUIT
WAITING FOR THE RIGHT TIME."

Shaa Wasmund

BE A GAMECHANGER

Enjoy the richness in being a gamechanger in your life, your family's life, your community and our world.

'Life's most persistent and urgent question is: "What are you doing for others?"'

— Dr Martin Luther King

BELIEVE BIGGER, BE BOLDER, BE A GAMECHANGER

This book has shown you how to start in rent to rent and how to create more freedom to live life on your terms. Its deeper message is to live in a bigger, bolder way to realise your dreams, with purpose. The true surprise and delight is that when you live this way, you become an inspiration and a catalyst for others, too.

GIVE BEFORE YOU'RE READY

These are the words that changed my perspective on giving, and they brought so much unexpected joy into our lives. I listened to Glen Carlson's Dent podcast with Steve Pipe,[28] and our decision to start giving *consistently* moved from 'one day' to that day. In the podcast, Glen and Steve talked about Pledge 1%[29]

This simple idea opened a door in my mind. We don't have to wait to give every day, in our businesses or in our lives. We can start right now. Perhaps we think we have to wait until we can give thousands – or even tens or hundreds of thousands – each time. Perhaps we think we need to hit a certain revenue target or income.

It isn't true. Most people reading this book can make the 1% Pledge. You could give:

- 1% of your income, or
- 1% of your revenue, or
- 1% of your profit, or
- 1% of whatever you choose.

The beauty of the 1% Pledge is that it feels possible. Today.

For most us, 1% feels too low and we're inspired to give more, to do more, to be more. We're inspired to be the change that we want to see. We're inspired to make the difference we can make to change our world. Even when I was on benefits at home with baby Alex, I could have honoured the 1% Pledge.

It would have amounted to 50p per week – and that's why some of us feel it's not worth it. We forget that we grow our giving over time. We forget that our simple actions can inspire others to give too. We forget that what seems a small amount to us can make a big difference to someone's life.

And giving is always a joy; it's such a privilege to be in the position to be a giver. It makes your heart sing. It makes your step spring. When you give, you're doing what we're all here to do: you're making the world a better place.

We were inspired to give every day in our business. Through the beauty and simplicity of B1G1 (Buy One Give One) we do[30]. B1G1 asks you to 'imagine you can change the world just by doing what you do every day'. B1G1 makes it easy to do that by creating an online platform where businesses can give to projects around the world. We now give every day as part of our business and it's become a wonderful part of what we do.

Whenever anyone buys this book, leaves a review on *The Rent 2 Rent Success Podcast*, or joins our Rent 2 Rent Kickstarter or Rent 2 Rent Superstar Programmes to change their life, we give to projects that are changing people's lives in other parts of the world. We're supporting projects in Malawi and Zimbabwe helping women to start businesses, and supporting children in Ghana and Kenya to be able to go to school. Through HMO Heaven, we give to the local charity Amazing Grace Spaces, which supports women who need houses.

It's a great feeling to know that, as we do our work, we're having a positive impact on others. We believe we're all here to leave our world better, and each of us does this in different ways. We are hugely grateful to have found, later in life, a way to truly enhance and inspire other people through what we do each day with our businesses.

Beginning with a 1% Pledge is a great way to start if you feel you're not quite ready for more yet.

If you only take one thing from this book, we want it to be that you should start giving now: by making the 1% Pledge or giving through B1G1, or in whatever way you choose. And start giving regularly, because you can. Most of us reading (and writing!) this book have the privilege of an abundant life, and it feels more abundant still when you share it.

Lots of love

Stephanie & Nicky

xx

"IF YOU'RE NOT MAKING SOMEONE ELSE'S LIFE BETTER, THEN YOU'RE WASTING YOUR TIME. YOUR LIFE WILL BECOME BETTER BY MAKING OTHER PEOPLE'S LIVES BETTER."

Will Smith

YOUR SUCCESS STORY

Your Future You is waiting

'When I stand before God at the end of my life, I would hope that I would not have a single bit of talent left, and could say, "I used everything you gave me."

Chadwick Boseman

YOU HAVE A DREAM

Honour it.

You are the only one who can.

Life is precious, but many of the things we prioritise aren't really important to us. That's why the Future You exercise we did together in Mindset Mastery is so important. Now you know what is truly important to you. Now you have your North Star. Commit to moving towards it. Commit to taking the steps, one at a time.

Nicky and I found the commitment part easy, but the action part is more difficult. Nicky listened to *Rich Dad, Poor Dad* in the Jamaican sunshine and thought, 'yes, I can do this'. Back in grey Beckenham, with bills on the table, it was harder to turn that commitment into actions. But if you want to be successful, that is what you must do.

Although you will doubt yourself at times, think like a gamechanger and always be there for you, no matter what; know you are resourceful and know you are unstoppable. The exact dreams you have came to you because you have the unique abilities to achieve them – otherwise, they wouldn't be your dreams.

Be compassionate to yourself. We're all human and have similar mind blocks. We don't need to beat ourselves up for making mistakes. We need to be compassionate and keep on getting up, knowing we have the capacity to improve.

Paths you may previously have thought were open only to people with resources you don't have *are* open to you. You can see examples of other busy people, other people with hesitations, other people with doubts, following our simple system and achieving extraordinary results.

People achieving the life-changing results they'd always dreamed of by bringing clarity to their goals and realising that a dream life is different for everyone. For many of us, it's simply buying ourselves the time freedom to live our lives on purpose and by design – to actually key a destination into our personal GPS and not just be blindly driving along without a map and seeing where we end up.

It's the kind of life-changing result that for Loise means she can now enjoy Christmas! That's after 20 years in accountancy in the City and 20 years of evermore stressful year-ends, when she would always miss out on Christmas, her favourite time of year. So many of us have jobs that rob us of the joy in our lives.

For Mark, it means he can spend more time with his children and be there for his family, for all those special moments you can never get back.

For Maria, it means she can involve her children in her business. She can show them what is possible and have the joy of her youngest saying, 'My mummy is a businesswoman.'

For us, the journey has changed us as people. We've grown so much. As well as loving (and sometimes bickering!) sisters, we've grown into people who truly value ourselves and each other. We're there more for our family – for our mum, Monica, who will move to Wales to join us, when she is ready.

For my son, Alex, I often wish I had known this world sooner and been able to bring him up in a world of abundance rather than scarcity. Now we understand the world of abundance, it's a joy to be able to share it with Alex and guide him in realising how much wealth he can grow and how much he can give.

We started out simply adding care… and found so much joy. We're constantly thinking about how we can give more, and finding that we also get more.

This is what we want for you. In fact, we want more for you than you can imagine right now. We want you to be surprised, delighted and excited when you see what you can do.

We want you to look back on today in a year's time and be glad you started.

If you have waited.

If you've hesitated.

If you've doubted.

Imagine your Future You, and do what you need to do today to move closer to that person you've reimagined for yourself. And enjoy every step of the way.

Don't let this book be entertainment.

Let it be an inspiration.

Let it be a catalyst.

Let it be your next step on your journey.

Believe Bigger, Be Bolder, Be a Gamechanger.

lots of love

Stephanie & Nicky xx

THE BEST FEELING IN THE WORLD!

'The best and most beautiful things in the world cannot be seen or even touched – they must be felt with the heart.'

Helen Keller

As the years go by, life teaches us the importance of community in achieving goals with impact far beyond you. The importance of connection and being near others who share your values and your goals.

And we'd love you to become part of the Rent 2 Rent Success Community. Join us in our free communities.

Join the Rent 2 Rent Success Facebook group:

rent2rentsuccess.com/group

Subscribe to the Rent 2 Rent Success YouTube channel:

rent2rentsuccess.com/youtube

Subscribe to *The Rent 2 Rent Success Podcast:*

rent2rentsuccess.com/podcast

And, of course, you can delve deeper and find out more with all the resources we've added to the **Rockstar Essentials website** for you:

rent2rentsuccess.com/essentials

Or perhaps you'd like to work more closely with us in the Rent 2 Rent Kickstarter Programme to get your first deal, and you want to book a Strategy Session with us to find out more about that:

rent2rentsuccess.com/strategy

We're so excited for you to take your greatness – especially if you didn't know it was there – and use it for good.

And we're so excited for us, too, as we know we will begin to receive emails saying this book was the catalyst. This book sparked your start in a new direction, and that is one of the best feelings in the world.

For you.

And for us.

To have spent so many years blind to possibility and then to be able to help others see theirs is such a joy. We want you to take action on your goals. We want you to write to us to tell us what a difference it's made to your life. And we wish you joy as you begin your rent to rent success story.

Please email us at **joy@rent2rentsuccess.com** to tell us your story.

'You can't go back and change the beginning, but you can start where you are and change the ending.'

CS Lewis

ENDNOTES

1 https://rent2rentsuccess.com/strategy

2 https://rent2rentsuccess.com/group

3 https://rent2rentsuccess.com/youtube

4 https://rent2rentsuccess.com/podcast

5 The PRS definition of rent to rent is available to download from our Rockstar Essentials website: https://rent2rentsuccess.com/essentials

6 https://rent2rentsuccess.com/essentials

7 Find out more about rent to rent start-up costs on our Rockstar Essentials website https://rent2rentsuccess.com/essentials

8 https://www.ons.gov.uk/employmentandlabourmarket/peopleinwork/earningsandworkinghours/datasets/averageweeklyearningsearn01

9 https://www.showhouse.co.uk/news/uk-needs-to-build-340000-new-homes-a-year-until-2031

10 https://blogs.lse.ac.uk/politicsandpolicy/housing-crisis-what-should-the-next-government-do/

11 http://researchbriefings.files.parliament.uk/documents/SN00708/SN00708.pdf

12 https://www.theguardian.com/money/2017/mar/02/home-ownership-in-england-at-a-30-year-low-official-figures-show

13 https://www.savills.com/research_articles/255800/300939-0/how-uk-residential-rents-behave-in-a-downturn

14 https://www.gov.uk/house-in-multiple-occupation-licence

15 https://www.mygov.scot/renting-your-property-out/registration/

16 https://rent2rentsuccess.com/essentials

17 https://rent2rentsuccess.com/essentials

18 https://rent2rentsuccess.com/essentials

19 Download the PRS Guide to Rent to Rent from https://rent2rentsuccess.com/essentials

20 https://rent2rentsuccess.com/essentials

21 https://rent2rentsuccess.com/essentials

22 https://rent2rentsuccess.com/essentials

23 https://rent2rentsuccess.com/essentials

24 England: https://www.gov.uk/government/publications/tenant-fees-act-2019-guidance.

Wales: https://gov.wales/letting-fees-guidance-landlords-and-letting-agents.

Scotland: https://www.gov.scot/publications/private-residential-tenancies-landlords-guide/pages/rent-and-other-charges/

25 https://rent2rentsuccess.com/essentials

26 https://amzn.to/38wlr6s

27 https://rent2rentsuccess.com/essentials

28 https://www.keypersonofinfluence.com/steve-pipe

29 https://pledge1percent.org

30 https://www.b1g1.com

ABOUT THE AUTHORS

Stephanie Taylor and Nicky Taylor are sisters, business partners and unlikely Co-Founders of HMO Heaven and Rent 2 Rent Success. Property has been life-changing for them and now they're passionate about sharing the ethical way to get started in property without having a huge amount of money to start.

Their journey has taken them from overworking and financial uncertainty to starting their own business in which they have:

- Attracted contracts worth over £2 million
- Built their own multi-million-pound property portfolio
- Created the Rent 2 Rent Success System which has helped hundreds of people get started in property and achieve success

They want to inspire more people to believe bigger, to be bolder and to be gamechangers for good. Being a gamechanger is part of the reason we're all here on the planet, to leave it a better place. They'd love to inspire you to get started in property and to make the 1% Pledge and start giving before you're ready.

Part of each sale of this book goes to providing homes for children in Kenya. The B1G1 (Buy One Give One) platform makes it effortless to give regularly to projects all over the world.

CONNECT WITH STEPHANIE & NICKY

Send us a message:

✉ joy@rent2rentsuccess.com

Join our facebook group:

f rent2rentsuccess.com/group

Follow us on Instagram:

📷 rent2rentsuccess.com/insta

Connect with us on LinkedIn:

in rent2rentsuccess.com/linkedin

See us on YouTube:

▶ rent2rentsuccess.com/youtube

Book a strategy call

📞 rent2rentsuccess.com/strategy

"YOU HAVE GREATNESS WITHIN YOU."

Les Brown

"YOU GET IN LIFE WHAT
YOU HAVE THE COURAGE
TO ASK FOR."

Oprah Winfrey

"IT ALWAYS SEEMS
IMPOSSIBLE,
UNTIL IT IS DONE."

Nelson Mandela

Printed in Great Britain
by Amazon